D0479140

HMH SCIENCE DIMENSIONS™
THE DIVERSITY OF LIVING THINGS

Module D

This Write-In Book belongs to

_____

Teacher/Room

_____

Houghton Mifflin Harcourt™

Consulting Authors

Michael A. DiSpezio

Global Educator
North Falmouth,
Massachusetts

Michael DiSpezio has authored many HMH instructional programs for Science and Mathematics. He has also authored numerous trade books and multimedia programs on various topics and hosted dozens of studio and location broadcasts for various organizations in the United States and worldwide. Most recently, he has been working with educators to provide strategies for implementing the Next Generation Science Standards, particularly the Science and Engineering Practices, Crosscutting Concepts, and the use of Evidence Notebooks. To all his projects, he brings his extensive background in science, his expertise in classroom teaching at the elementary, middle, and high school levels, and his deep experience in producing interactive and engaging instructional materials.

Marjorie Frank

Science Writer and Content-Area Reading Specialist
Brooklyn, New York

An educator and linguist by training, a writer and poet by nature, Marjorie Frank has authored and designed a generation of instructional materials in all subject areas, including past HMH Science programs. Her other credits include authoring science issues of an award-winning children's magazine, writing game-based digital assessments, developing blended learning materials for young children, and serving as instructional designer and coauthor of pioneering school-to-work software. In addition, she has served on the adjunct faculty of Hunter, Manhattan, and Brooklyn Colleges, teaching courses in science methods, literacy, and writing. For *HMH Science Dimensions™*, she has guided the development of our K–2 strands and our approach to making connections between NGSS and Common Core ELA/literacy standards.

Acknowledgments for Covers

Cover credits: (fern leaf head) ©hafizismail/Fotolia; (fern fossils) ©Science Stock Photography/Science Source.

Section Header Master Art: (human cells, illustration) ©Sebastian Kaulitzki/Science Photo Library/Corbis.

Copyright © 2018 by Houghton Mifflin Harcourt Publishing Company

All rights reserved. No part of this work may be reproduced or transmitted in any form or by any means, electronic or mechanical, including photocopying or recording, or by any information storage and retrieval system, without the prior written permission of the copyright owner unless such copying is expressly permitted by federal copyright law. Requests for permission to make copies of any part of the work should be submitted through our Permissions website at https://customercare.hmhco.com/contactus/Permissions.html or mailed to Houghton Mifflin Harcourt Publishing Company, Attn: Intellectual Property Licensing, 9400 Southpark Center Loop, Orlando, Florida 32819-8647.

Printed in the U.S.A.

ISBN   978-0-544-86097-1

2 3 4 5 6 7 8 9 10   0928   25 24 23 22 21 20 19 18 17

4500678002   A B C D E F G

If you have received these materials as examination copies free of charge, Houghton Mifflin Harcourt Publishing Company retains title to the materials and they may not be resold. Resale of examination copies is strictly prohibited.

Possession of this publication in print format does not entitle users to convert this publication, or any portion of it, into electronic format.

© Houghton Mifflin Harcourt • Image Credits: (all) HMH

Michael R. Heithaus, PhD

Dean, College of Arts, Sciences & Education Professor, Department of Biological Sciences
Florida International University
Miami, Florida

Mike Heithaus joined the FIU Biology Department in 2003 and has served as Director of the Marine Sciences Program and Executive Director of the School of Environment, Arts, and Society, which brings together the natural and social sciences and humanities to develop solutions to today's environmental challenges. He now serves as Dean of the College of Arts, Sciences & Education. His research focuses on predator-prey interactions and the ecological importance of large marine species. He has helped to guide the development of Life Science content in *HMH Science Dimensions™*, with a focus on strategies for teaching challenging content as well as the science and engineering practices of analyzing data and using computational thinking.

Cary I. Sneider, PhD

Associate Research Professor
Portland State University
Portland, Oregon

While studying astrophysics at Harvard, Cary Sneider volunteered to teach in an Upward Bound program and discovered his real calling as a science teacher. After teaching middle and high school science in Maine, California, Costa Rica, and Micronesia, he settled for nearly three decades at Lawrence Hall of Science in Berkeley, California, where he developed skills in curriculum development and teacher education. Over his career, Cary directed more than 20 federal, state, and foundation grant projects and was a writing team leader for the Next Generation Science Standards. He has been instrumental in ensuring *HMH Science Dimensions™* meets the high expectations of the NGSS and provides an effective three-dimensional learning experience for all students.

Program Advisors

Paul D. Asimow, PhD
Eleanor and John R. McMillan Professor of Geology and Geochemistry
California Institute of Technology
Pasadena, California

Joanne Bourgeois
Professor Emerita
Earth & Space Sciences
University of Washington
Seattle, WA

Dr. Eileen Cashman
Professor
Humboldt State University
Arcata, California

Elizabeth A. De Stasio, PhD
Raymond J. Herzog Professor of Science
Lawrence University
Appleton, Wisconsin

Perry Donham, PhD
Lecturer
Boston University
Boston, Massachusetts

Shila Garg, PhD
Emerita Professor of Physics
Former Dean of Faculty & Provost
The College of Wooster
Wooster, Ohio

Tatiana A. Krivosheev, PhD
Professor of Physics
Clayton State University
Morrow, Georgia

Mark B. Moldwin, PhD
Professor of Space Sciences and Engineering
University of Michigan
Ann Arbor, Michigan

Ross H. Nehm
Stony Brook University (SUNY)
Stony Brook, NY

Kelly Y. Neiles, PhD
Assistant Professor of Chemistry
St. Mary's College of Maryland
St. Mary's City, Maryland

John Nielsen-Gammon, PhD
Regents Professor
Department of Atmospheric Sciences
Texas A&M University
College Station, Texas

Dr. Sten Odenwald
Astronomer
NASA Goddard Spaceflight Center
Greenbelt, Maryland

Bruce W. Schafer
Executive Director
Oregon Robotics Tournament & Outreach Program
Beaverton, Oregon

Barry A. Van Deman
President and CEO
Museum of Life and Science
Durham, North Carolina

Kim Withers, PhD
Assistant Professor
Texas A&M University-Corpus Christi
Corpus Christi, Texas

Adam D. Woods, PhD
Professor
California State University, Fullerton
Fullerton, California

© Houghton Mifflin Harcourt • Image Credits: (all) HMH

Classroom Reviewers

Cynthia Book, PhD
John Barrett Middle School
Carmichael, California

Katherine Carter, MEd
Fremont Unified School District
Fremont, California

Theresa Hollenbeck, MEd
Winston Churchill Middle School
Carmichael, California

Kathryn S. King
Science and AVID Teacher
Norwood Jr. High School
Sacramento, California

Donna Lee
Science/STEM Teacher
Junction Ave. K8
Livermore, California

Rebecca S. Lewis
Science Teacher
North Rockford Middle School
Rockford, Michigan

Bryce McCourt
8th Grade Science Teacher/Middle School Curriculum Chair
Cudahy Middle School
Cudahy, Wisconsin

Sarah Mrozinski
Teacher
St. Sebastian School
Milwaukee, Wisconsin

Raymond Pietersen
Science Program Specialist
Elk Grove Unified School District
Elk Grove, California

© Houghton Mifflin Harcourt

You are a scientist!
You are naturally curious.

© Houghton Mifflin Harcourt • Image Credits: © Hero Images/Getty Images

Have you ever wondered . . .

- why is it difficult to catch a fly?
- how a new island can appear in an ocean?
- how to design a great tree house?
- how a spacecraft can send messages across the solar system?

HMH SCIENCE DIMENSIONS™

will *SPARK* your curiosity!

AND prepare you for

✓	tomorrow
✓	next year
✓	college or career
✓	life!

Where do you see yourself in 15 years?

© Houghton Mifflin Harcourt • Image Credits: (t) ©Hill Street Studios/Blend Images/ Corbis; (cl) ©Adam Gregor/Shutterstock; (c) ©Laura Doss/FancyCorbis; (cr) ©Design Pics Inc./Alamy; (bl) ©Steve Debenport/Getty Images; (bc) ©Monkey Business Images/ Shutterstock; (br) ©Blend Images/Alamy Images

Observe

Collect Data

Be a scientist.
Work like real scientists work.

Analyze

© Houghton Mifflin Harcourt • Image Credits: (t) ©Hero Images/Getty Images; (b) ©Tetra Images/Corbis

Be an engineer.
Solve problems like engineers do.

Define Problems

Test Solutions

STEM

© Houghton Mifflin Harcourt • Image Credits: (t) ©alexey_boldin/Fotolia; (b) ©Ariel Skelley/Blend Images/Corbis

Gather Information

Think Critically

Explain your world.
Start by asking questions.

Conduct Investigations

© Houghton Mifflin Harcourt • Image Credits: (t) ©Hero Images/Fancy/Corbis; (tr) ©Tyler Olson/Shutterstock; (b) ©PhotoAlto/Alamy

Collaborate

Develop Explanations

Construct Arguments

There's more than one way to the answer. What's YOURS?

© Houghton Mifflin Harcourt • Image Credits: (t) ©Antenna/stop/Corbis; (b) ©Fuse/Getty Images

YOUR Program

Write-In Book:

- a brand-new and innovative textbook that will guide you through your next generation curriculum, including your hands-on lab program

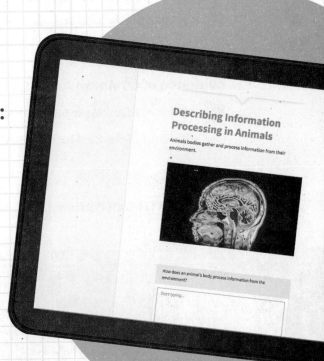

Describing Information Processing in Animals

Animals bodies gather and process information from their environment.

How does an animal's body process information from the environment?

Start typing...

Interactive Online Student Edition:

- a complete online version of your textbook enriched with videos, interactivities, animations, simulations, and room to enter data, draw, and store your work

More tools are available online to help you practice and learn science, including:

- Hands-On Labs
- Science and Engineering Practices Handbook
- Crosscutting Concepts Handbook
- English Language Arts Handbook
- Math Handbook

© Houghton Mifflin Harcourt • Image Credits: (t) ©Roman Sigaev/Shutterstock; (b) ©Anatoliy Babiy/Pressureua/Dreamstime

Contents

The History of Life on Earth

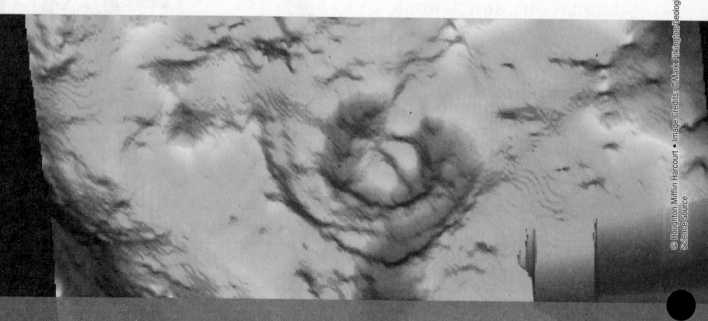

Long ago, a meteorite hit Earth in the Gulf of Mexico, causing large-scale changes to Earth's environment. The crater it left behind was over 100 miles wide.

© Houghton Mifflin Harcourt • Image Credits: ©Mark Pilkington/Geological Survey of Canada/Science Source

UNIT 2

73

Evolution

The African bush viper lives in tropical forests. Its scales
help it camouflage within the bright green foliage.

© Houghton Mifflin Harcourt o Image Credits: ©Mark Kostich/iStock/Getty Images Plus/ Getty Images

UNIT 3

Human Influence on Inheritance

The color, spot pattern, shape, and size of guppies can be emphasized through artificial selection.

© Houghton Mifflin Harcourt • Image Credit: ©underworld111/iStock/Getty Images Plus/ Getty Images

Whether you are in the lab or in the field, you are responsible for your own safety and the safety of others. To fulfill these responsibilities and avoid accidents, be aware of the safety of your classmates as well as your own safety at all times. Take your lab work and fieldwork seriously, and behave appropriately. Elements of safety to keep in mind are shown below and on the following pages.

© Houghton Mifflin Harcourt • Image Credits: (l) ©Houghton Mifflin Harcourt (r) ©Alistair Berg/DigitalVision/Getty Images

Safety in the Lab

- [ ] Be sure you understand the materials, your procedure, and the safety rules before you start an investigation in the lab.
- [ ] Know where to find and how to use fire extinguishers, eyewash stations, shower stations, and emergency power shutoffs.
- [ ] Use proper safety equipment. Always wear personal protective equipment, such as eye protection and gloves, when setting up labs, during labs, and when cleaning up.
- [ ] Do not begin until your teacher has told you to start. Follow directions.
- [ ] Keep the lab neat and uncluttered. Clean up when you are finished. Report all spills to your teacher immediately. Watch for slip/fall and trip/fall hazards.
- [ ] If you or another student are injured in any way, tell your teacher immediately, even if the injury seems minor.
- [ ] Do not take any food or drink into the lab. Never take any chemicals out of the lab.

Safety in the Field

- [ ] Be sure you understand the goal of your fieldwork and the proper way to carry out the investigation before you begin fieldwork.
- [ ] Use proper safety equipment and personal protective equipment, such as eye protection, that suits the terrain and the weather.
- [ ] Follow directions, including appropriate safety procedures as provided by your teacher.
- [ ] Do not approach or touch wild animals. Do not touch plants unless instructed by your teacher to do so. Leave natural areas as you found them.
- [ ] Stay with your group.
- [ ] Use proper accident procedures, and let your teacher know about a hazard in the environment or an accident immediately, even if the hazard or accident seems minor.

Safety Symbols

To highlight specific types of precautions, the following symbols are used throughout the lab program. Remember that no matter what safety symbols you see within each lab, all safety rules should be followed at all times.

Dress Code

- Wear safety goggles (or safety glasses as appropriate for the activity) at all times in the lab as directed. If chemicals get into your eye, flush your eyes immediately for a minimum of 15 minutes.
- Do not wear contact lenses in the lab.
- Do not look directly at the sun or any intense light source or laser.
- Wear appropriate protective non-latex gloves as directed.
- Wear an apron or lab coat at all times in the lab as directed.
- Tie back long hair, secure loose clothing, and remove loose jewelry. Remove acrylic nails when working with active flames.
- Do not wear open-toed shoes, sandals, or canvas shoes in the lab.

Glassware and Sharp Object Safety

- Do not use chipped or cracked glassware.
- Use heat-resistant glassware for heating or storing hot materials.
- Notify your teacher immediately if a piece of glass breaks.
- Use extreme care when handling any sharp or pointed instruments.
- Do not cut an object while holding the object unsupported in your hands. Place the object on a suitable cutting surface, and always cut in a direction away from your body.

Chemical Safety

- If a chemical gets on your skin, on your clothing, or in your eyes, rinse it immediately for a minimum of 15 minutes (using the shower, faucet, or eyewash station), and alert your teacher.
- Do not clean up spilled chemicals unless your teacher directs you to do so.
- Do not inhale any gas or vapor unless directed to do so by your teacher. If you are instructed to note the odor of a substance, wave the fumes toward your nose with your hand. This is called wafting. Never put your nose close to the source of the odor.
- Handle materials that emit vapors or gases in a well-ventilated area.
- Keep your hands away from your face while you are working on any activity.

© Houghton Mifflin Harcourt

Safety Symbols, continued

Electrical Safety

- Do not use equipment with frayed electrical cords or loose plugs.
- Do not use electrical equipment near water or when clothing or hands are wet.
- Hold the plug housing when you plug in or unplug equipment. Do not pull on the cord.
- Use only GFI-protected electrical receptacles.

Heating and Fire Safety

- Be aware of any source of flames, sparks, or heat (such as flames, heating coils, or hot plates) before working with any flammable substances.
- Know the location of the lab's fire extinguisher and fire-safety blankets.
- Know your school's fire-evacuation routes.
- If your clothing catches on fire, walk to the lab shower to put out the fire. Do not run.
- Never leave a hot plate unattended while it is turned on or while it is cooling.
- Use tongs or appropriately insulated holders when handling heated objects.
- Allow all equipment to cool before storing it.

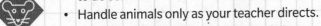

Plant and Animal Safety

- Do not eat any part of a plant.
- Do not pick any wild plant unless your teacher instructs you to do so.
- Handle animals only as your teacher directs.
- Treat animals carefully and respectfully.
- Wash your hands throughly with soap and water after handling any plant or animal.

Cleanup

- Clean all work surfaces and protective equipment as directed by your teacher.
- Dispose of hazardous materials or sharp objects only as directed by your teacher.
- Wash your hands throughly with soap and water before you leave the lab or after any activity.

© Houghton Mifflin Harcourt

Student Safety Quiz

Circle the letter of the BEST answer.

1. Before starting an investigation or lab procedure, you should
   A. try an experiment of your own
   B. open all containers and packages
   C. read all directions and make sure you understand them
   D. handle all the equipment to become familiar with it

2. At the end of any activity you should
   A. wash your hands thoroughly with soap and water before leaving the lab
   B. cover your face with your hands
   C. put on your safety goggles
   D. leave hot plates switched on

3. If you get hurt or injured in any way, you should
   A. tell your teacher immediately
   B. find bandages or a first aid kit
   C. go to your principal's office
   D. get help after you finish the lab

4. If your glassware is chipped or broken, you should
   A. use it only for solid materials
   B. give it to your teacher for recycling or disposal
   C. put it back into the storage cabinet
   D. increase the damage so that it is obvious

5. If you have unused chemicals after finishing a procedure, you should
   A. pour them down a sink or drain
   B. mix them all together in a bucket
   C. put them back into their original containers
   D. dispose of them as directed by your teacher

6. If electrical equipment has a frayed cord, you should
   A. unplug the equipment by pulling the cord
   B. let the cord hang over the side of a counter or table
   C. tell your teacher about the problem immediately
   D. wrap tape around the cord to repair it

7. If you need to determine the odor of a chemical or a solution, you should
   A. use your hand to bring fumes from the container to your nose
   B. bring the container under your nose and inhale deeply
   C. tell your teacher immediately
   D. use odor-sensing equipment

8. When working with materials that might fly into the air and hurt someone's eye, you should wear
   A. goggles
   B. an apron
   C. gloves
   D. a hat

9. Before doing experiments involving a heat source, you should know the location of the
   A. door
   B. window
   C. fire extinguisher
   D. overhead lights

10. If you get chemicals in your eye you should
   A. wash your hands immediately
   B. put the lid back on the chemical container
   C. wait to see if your eye becomes irritated
   D. use the eyewash station right away, for a minimum of 15 minutes

Go online to view the Lab Safety Handbook for additional information.

© Houghton Mifflin Harcourt

The History of Life on Earth

This image shows an artist's impression of early Earth. Millions of years later, the first forms of life appeared.

© Houghton Mifflin Harcourt • Image Credits: ©Mark Garlick/Science Photo Library/ Getty Images

The history of life on Earth is a fascinating mystery, complete with intriguing plants and animals and life and death struggles. Earth has been around for a *very* long time—4.6 billion years! How do we know so much about the history of life on Earth? In this unit, you will learn how scientists use evidence found in fossils and rocks, along with an understanding of natural processes and scientific principles, to unravel this extraordinary mystery.

Why It Matters

Here are some questions to consider as you work through the unit. Can you answer any of the questions now? Revisit these questions at the end of the unit to apply what you discover.

Question	Notes
Why is the variety of life on Earth now different than it was in Earth's past?	
What extinct organisms once lived in your area?	
What can be learned by studying a fossil?	
Why do some types of organisms have similar appearances, while other types of organisms appear very different?	
How is a common ancestor in a human family tree similar to a common ancestor among different species?	
How are dogs more similar to wolves than they are to cats?	

© Houghton Mifflin Harcourt

Unit Starter: Comparing Anatomical Structures

One way that scientists study relationships among organisms is to look for anatomical similarities that they share. An organism's anatomy includes its physical features. For example, these three organisms all have wings, but they are anatomically different. Use the photos to answer the following questions.

A dragonfly rests on a branch. Notice the structure of its wings.

A green-crowned brilliant hummingbird lands on a flower in Ecuador.

This sandhill crane extends its wings to land in a field in New Mexico.

1. Study the wing structure of these organisms. The wings of the hummingbird are more similar to the wings of the *crane / dragonfly*.

2. Based on anatomical similarities, the hummingbird is likely *more / less* closely related to the crane than the dragonfly.

Go online to download the Unit Project Worksheet to help you plan your project.

Unit Project

All in the Family

Many people are fascinated by their family history and construct a family tree to keep track of their ancestors and living relatives. Your task is to construct a family tree for an animal species. Use anatomical evidence from the fossil record and living organisms to identify the ancestors and closest living relatives of your organism.

© Houghton Mifflin Harcourt • Image Credits: (t) ©asfloro/Fotolia; (c) ©Glenn Bartley/All Canada Photos/Getty Images; (b) ©Robbie George/National Geographic/Getty Images

The Fossil Record

About 125 million years ago, this mosquito got stuck in sticky tree sap. Over time, the sap hardened around the insect, forming amber, which preserved the mosquito's body.

By the end of this lesson . . .

you will be able to explain how fossil data can be used to provide evidence of the history of life on Earth.

© Houghton Mifflin Harcourt • Image Credits: ©Marc DEVILLE/Gamma-Rapho/Getty Images

Go online to view the digital version of the Hands-On Lab for this lesson and to download additional lab resources.

CAN YOU EXPLAIN IT?

How can fossils help us learn about a whale that lived 40 million years ago?

This model shows what the whale *Dorudon atrox* may have looked like when it was alive. The model is based on data gathered from its fossils such as these from Whale Valley in Egypt.

Explore ONLINE!

© Houghton Mifflin Harcourt • Image Credits: (t) ©A&E Television Networks/The Image Bank/Getty Images; (b) ©A&E Television Networks/The Image Bank/Getty Images

1. What observations and inferences from the fossils might have been used to build the computer model?

2. What similarities and differences do you observe between the fossil remains and the computer model of the whale?

EVIDENCE NOTEBOOK As you explore this lesson, gather evidence to help explain how fossil data can be used to learn about an ancient whale species.

Explaining Fossil Formation

We know a lot about the history of life on Earth from studying fossils. **Fossils** are the remains or traces of once-living organisms. Fossils form when specific conditions occur that preserve an organism's remains. In most cases, an organism's remains are eaten, scattered, dissolved by water, or decomposed before they can be preserved.

How Fossils Can Form

The most common fossils formed when the remains of dead animals were covered by sediment. Usually only the hard parts of the animal fossilized, but sometimes the soft parts fossilized too.

An injured *Dorudon* nears death.

The *Dorudon* dies and sinks to the ocean floor.

Scavengers may eat the soft tissues or the tissues may decompose.

The skeleton gets covered by sediments.

More sediment buries the entire skeleton.

Layers of sediment build up. They turn to rock. The ocean floor becomes dry land due to tectonic changes.

Erosion exposes the rock layer containing the *Dorudon* bones.

3. Review the fossilization process in the diagram. Which of these conditions might prevent a dead organism from being preserved?

  A. being trapped in tree sap

  B. being eaten or decomposing

  C. being dissolved by water

  D. being buried by sediments

Ways Fossils Can Form

It is rare for an organism's remains to form a fossil. Many processes can prevent fossil formation. The remains of less than one percent of all the species that ever lived fossilized. Fossils form most often when an organism's remains are quickly buried by sediments. That is why most fossils are found in sedimentary rock. Quick burial by sediments occurs more often in rivers, lakes, and oceans than it does on land. Therefore, water-dwelling organisms are more likely to be fossilized than land animals.

Fossils may form from an organism's bones, teeth, or shells. They may also form from activity. Fossils of soft-bodied animals, such as jellyfish, are rare, but they do exist. Proteins and genetic material may also fossilize. For example, scientists identified certain cell structures in fossilized feathers that help them determine the color of the feathers.

© Houghton Mifflin Harcourt

Types of Fossils

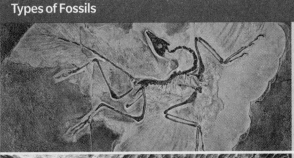

Permineralized fossil *Permineralization* happens when an organism's tissues are replaced by minerals from water. These minerals form a hard, three-dimensional "copy" of the original organism. The bones and feathers of this *Archaeopteryx* are permineralized.

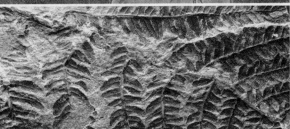

Carbonized fossil A *carbonized fossil* forms when an organism, usually a plant, is quickly buried and flattened by the enormous pressure of sediments built up above it. Most of the nitrogen, oxygen, and hydrogen that made up the organism gets removed. Only the carbon from the organism remains as a thin, black film. These fern leaves are carbonized.

Amber fossil A very long time ago, this spider got stuck in sticky tree sap. It became sealed in as the sap covered its entire body. Over time, the sap hardened into a material called *amber*. The organism was preserved in the amber. Insects, spiders, and even feathers can become fossilized in amber.

Cast and mold fossils After an organism's tissues decompose, an impression of its body shape can be left in sediment. This impression is called a *mold fossil*. Water may seep in and fill the impression. Minerals in the water harden to form a *cast fossil*. Both cast and mold fossils of shelled animals called *brachiopods* are shown in the photo.

Trace fossil A *trace fossil* is a record of the activity of an organism. It may be footprints, such as these left by *Brontosaurus*, or it may be a burrow, scratches, or fossilized dung. Trace fossils are categorized by the activity that created them. Such activities include feeding, walking, running, or burrowing.

Tar pit fossil A *tar pit* is an area where sticky, thick liquid called *asphalt* seeps up to Earth's surface. This water beetle was found in the La Brea tar pits, Los Angeles, California. The beetle died, along with other trapped animals, and tar covered its body. The tar dissolved the soft body parts, but preserved the hard parts, such as the exoskeletons and bones.

Frozen remains Frozen remains, such as those of this baby woolly mammoth, form when an organism becomes trapped in some way, dies, and then is quickly frozen. As long as the surroundings stay frozen, the fossil will also remain frozen. Freezing preserves much of the organism, including genetic material. This mammoth calf, named Lyuba by researchers, still has her trunk, fur, and internal organs.

© Houghton Mifflin Harcourt • Image Credits: (1) ©Naturfoto Honal/Corbis Documentary/Getty Images; (2) ©DEA/G. CIGOLINI/De Agostini/Getty Images; (3) ©ullstein bild/Getty Images; (4) ©L. K. Broman/Science Source; (5) ©Francois Gohier/Science Source; (6) ©Colin Keates/Corbis Documentary/Getty Images; (7) ©SVF2/Universal Images Group/Getty Images

4. Observe the trace fossil and the permineralized fossil. What observations might scientists be able to collect from each type of fossil?

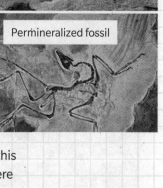

Trace fossil

Permineralized fossil

Case Study: The Morrison Formation

About 150 million years ago (mya), the area shown on the map was a large flood plain with many rivers. The conditions in this ancient flood plain environment were favorable for the quick burial of organisms that died there. It is now one of the most fossil-rich areas in the world. Many fossils of the organisms that died in this area are scattered and incomplete because of the movement of rivers, but not all were destroyed. Other locations have complete fossils.

The Morrison Formation

The Morrison Formation is a large area of sedimentary rock that is the most concentrated source of fossils in the United States. Some fossils are complete; others are mixed and jumbled together.

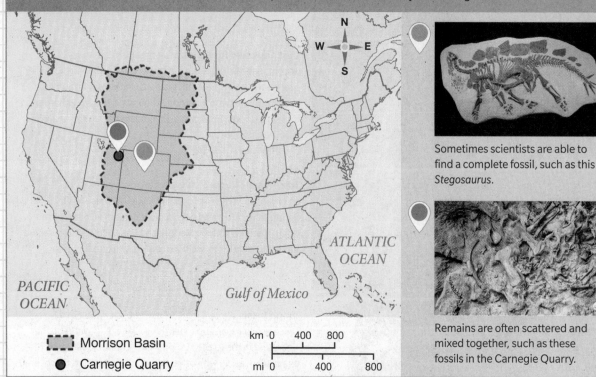

N
W   E
S

ATLANTIC OCEAN

PACIFIC OCEAN

Gulf of Mexico

- - - Morrison Basin
● Carnegie Quarry

km 0   400   800
mi 0   400   800

Sometimes scientists are able to find a complete fossil, such as this *Stegosaurus*.

Remains are often scattered and mixed together, such as these fossils in the Carnegie Quarry.

5. Does the high concentration of fossils in the Morrison Formation mean that more organisms lived here 150 mya compared to other parts of the country? Explain your reasoning.

© Houghton Mifflin Harcourt • Image Credits: (t) ©Francois Gohier/Science Source; (tc) ©Naturfoto Honal/Corbis Documentary/Getty Images; (bc) ©Francois Gohier/Western Paleontological Labs/Science Source; (b) ©Martin Bache/Alamy

![Hands-On Lab icon]

Hands-On Lab
Model Fossil Formation

You will model the process of fossil formation and make your own cast fossil. You will exchange fossils with another group and make inferences about the items that made the other group's fossil.

Procedure and Analysis

STEP 1 Select two or more items to make a cast fossil.

STEP 2 Press the clay to form a flat, thick surface. Make it thick enough so that you can push your chosen items into it.

STEP 3 Arrange the items on the clay. Then press them into the clay to make a detailed impression. What do the modeling clay and the small objects represent in this model of a fossilization process?

MATERIALS
- modeling clay
- various items to form cast fossils
- white glue

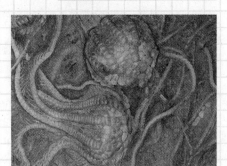

This cast fossil of *Uintacrinus socialis*, an extinct marine animal, gives an impression of the size and shape of the organism when it was alive.

STEP 4 Carefully remove the items from the clay. Try not to disturb the impressions. The clay impression forms a mold.

STEP 5 Fill the mold with white glue and let it dry.

STEP 6 When the glue has dried, peel it back. The dried glue shape is a cast of your items.

STEP 7 Exchange cast fossils with another group. Make inferences about the items used to make their cost fossils, and explain your reasoning.

STEP 8 Confirm what items were used to make the trace fossils that you analyzed.

STEP 9 What were you able to infer from the cast fossil you analyzed? Did your inferences correctly reflect the original items that made the fossil?

© Houghton Mifflin Harcourt • Image Credits: ©Kevin Schafer/Alamy Images

STEP 10 What about the "fossilization process" made it difficult to accurately or completely identify the original item?

___

EVIDENCE NOTEBOOK

6. The fossil shown at the beginning of the lesson is from an extinct whale. Under what environmental conditions did that fossil probably form? What can be learned from that type of fossil? Record your evidence.

Analyze Conditions for Fossilization

Fossils of some species are very common and well known to scientists, while others are rare. This difference is due in part to the environment in which the organisms lived and died. For example, there are far more marine fossils than land fossils. One reason for the greater number of marine fossils is that many marine organisms have shells. The shells are very hard, do not decay easily, and are rarely eaten by other organisms. In contrast, soft-bodied animals, such as slugs, lack hard body parts. The bodies would quickly decay or be eaten by scavengers before they could be covered with sediments.

Marine fossils, such as these scallop and oyster fossils, formed in the sediment of the shallow sea in which they lived.

7. Which conditions most likely existed at the location in which these fossilized organisms once lived to enable so many fossils to form? Choose all correct answers.

   A. The ocean waters were very warm.

   B. Many soft-bodied organisms lived there.

   C. Many hard-bodied organisms lived there.

   D. Sediments quickly covered the dead organisms, hiding them from scavengers.

8. Which fossil record would likely show more diversity, land-living organisms or marine organisms? Explain your answer.

   _____

   _____

   _____

   _____

   _____

© Houghton Mifflin Harcourt • Image Credits: ©Stephanie Friedman/Houghton Mifflin Harcourt

Studying the Ages of Fossils

No one was around to observe fossils forming or to see other natural processes occurring millions of years ago. Yet we can infer what happed in the past based on what we know about the natural processes that occur today. Scientists assume that the geologic events and phenomena that happen today also happened in the past and that they apply everywhere in nature. This scientific principle is called *uniformitarianism*. We can use these assumptions to interpret fossil data.

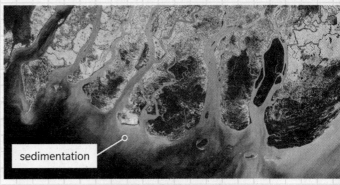

sedimentation

This satellite photo shows rivers that carry water and sediment out to sea. Soil and rock particles are eroded from the riverbanks by water, carried down the rivers, and deposited in the sea, which causes sediment to build up.

For example, scientists know that today, sedimentary rock forms when sediments carried by air, ice, water, or gravity are deposited in layers in a new location. Over time, the weight of the sediment layers puts pressure on the layers below them, and sedimentary rock forms. So we can assume that sedimentation and sedimentary rock formation in ancient seas occurred in a similar way.

9. How does knowledge of sedimentary rock formation help us to understand fossils?

Relative Ages of Rock Layers

Sedimentary rock forms in layers. The *law of superposition* states that in a sequence of undisturbed sedimentary rocks, the oldest layers are at the bottom and the youngest ones are at the top. The oldest layers are deposited first. Over time, these layers are buried as new sediment gets deposited on top of the existing layers. This "layering" of rock is very noticeable in the Grand Canyon because several of the rock layers are different colors. By studying the layers in undisturbed sedimentary rocks, scientists can find the relative age of each layer. The *relative age* of a rock layer relates to whether that layer is older or younger than other rock layers.

Grand Canyon

10. The rock layer on the top of the Grand Canyon is the youngest / oldest because it was deposited most recently / in the distant past. Layers in the middle are younger / older than the surface layer. The layer farthest down is the youngest / oldest because it was deposited most recently / the earliest.

© Houghton Mifflin Harcourt • Image Credits: (t) ©NASA Earth Observatory; (b) ©markrhiggins/iStock/Getty Images Plus/Getty Images

Geologic Columns

Scientists can also compare the relative ages of rock layers in different areas. This comparison is done using a geologic column. A *geologic column* is an ordered arrangement of rock layers that is based on the relative ages of the rocks, with the oldest rocks at the bottom of the column. It is made by piecing together different rock sequences from different areas. A geologic column therefore represents an ideal image of a rock layer sequence that doesn't actually exist in any one place on Earth. It is a conceptual model that shows the order of different rock layers and fossils over time. Scientists can compare a rock layer from one location with a similar layer in a geologic column that has the same fossils or that has the same relative position. If the two layers match, then they probably formed around the same time.

11. Geologic columns are models that are used to organize and study Earth's geologic history and fossil record. How do they relate to the principle of uniformitarianism?

Absolute Ages of Rock Layers

Sometimes scientists want to know the absolute, or actual, age of rocks or fossils. Scientists know that certain unstable particles that make up matter in rocks and living organisms change into different stable particles at a constant rate. This process is called *radioactive decay*. Some particles decay, or break down, in just hours. Other particles decay over millions of years. For example, one type of particle in igneous rock is radioactive uranium. When igneous rock forms, it contains a small amount of radioactive uranium. Over millions of years, these uranium particles decay to form lead particles.

Scientists know the rate at which particular radioactive particles decay. The time needed for half of a sample of a radioactive substance to decay is called the *half-life*. Because each radioactive substance decays at a specific, constant rate, each radioactive substance has a specific half-life. The half-life of radioactive uranium is 704 million years. That means it takes 704 million years for half of a rock's uranium to change to lead.

Timeline of the Breakdown of Uranium to Lead over Three Half-Lives

▲ Uranium   ▲ Lead

0 years This igneous rock just formed. It contains unstable uranium particles. At this time, none of the uranium has become lead.

704 million years One half-life, or 704 million years, has passed. That means half of the unstable uranium has changed into a more stable form of lead.

1,408 million years Another half-life has passed. That means that half of the remaining uranium particles have changed into lead.

2,112 million years This pattern continues. At any point in time, scientists can measure the amounts of uranium and lead in the rock to calculate the age of the rock.

© Houghton Mifflin Harcourt

Radiometric Dating

The method of finding the absolute age of rock based on comparing the amounts of unstable, radioactive particles to stable particles in a sample is called **radiometric dating**. For example, at any point in time, scientists can measure the amount of uranium and lead in a sample of igneous rock and find the rock's age.

Fossils do not contain the unstable particles that are used in radiometric dating. So scientists cannot use radiometric dating directly on fossils. Instead they use radiometric dating on igneous rock layers. Igneous rock forms from cooled magma and lava. Fossils are not found in igneous rock because the high temperature of the molten rock destroys the remains. Scientists determine the age of fossils by first identifying the age of the igneous rock layers above and below the fossils.

Data from igneous rock layers above a fossil provide an absolute age for the rock that formed after the fossil formed. Data from the igneous rock layers below provide the absolute age for the rock that formed before the fossil formed. This information gives scientists a timespan in which the fossilized organism lived.

12. A fossil was found in a sedimentary rock layer. The igneous layer directly above the sedimentary layer was analyzed for radioactive uranium. You found equal amounts of uranium and lead in the igneous sample. This means that the relative / absolute age of the igneous layer is 704 million years, and the age of the fossil in the sedimentary rock layer below is older / younger than 704 million years.

Index Fossils

Scientists observe that certain types of fossils appear only in certain layers of rock on Earth and only for a short span of time. By finding the age of igneous rock layers above and below these fossil layers, scientists can determine the timespan during which the fossilized organisms lived. These fossils, called *index fossils*, can then be used to estimate the absolute age of all the rock layers in which they are found. To be an index fossil, the organism from which the fossil formed must have lived during a relatively short geologic timespan. The fossils must be relatively common and must be found over a large area on Earth. Index fossils must also have features that make them easy to distinguish from other fossils

Nerinea is an extinct genus of sea snail. They were alive during the late Jurassic Period. They are index fossils for the Jurassic Period.

© Houghton Mifflin Harcourt • Image Credits: ©DEA/G. CIGOLINI/Universal Images Group/ NewsCom

Determining the Age of Fossils

Scientists can determine the age of a fossil by analyzing the rock layers above and below the fossil layer.

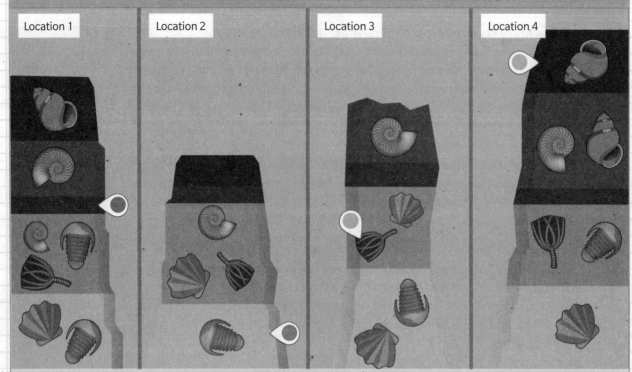

Location 1   Location 2   Location 3   Location 4

Use of igneous rock to date fossils Scientists can identify the age of igneous rock layers by radiometric dating. Layers of igneous rock do not contain fossils because they form from cooled magma. The high temperatures of magma would destroy the remains.

Index fossils This fossilized sea creature, called a graptolite, is found in only one layer in several different locations, which makes it a good index fossil. Index fossils are useful in identifying the age of other rock strata as well as other fossils.

Oldest layers The oldest layers are found at the bottom of a sequence of rock layers. Fossils found in this layer will also be the oldest. Many of the earliest fossils, such as trilobites, look very different from organisms that are alive today.

Most recent layers The topmost layer is the youngest, since it was most recently created by geologic processes. Fossils found in rock layers closest to the surface are from organisms that lived closer to the present day. Some of these fossils may look quite similar to living organisms.

13. Language SmArts Suppose the index fossil in the diagram has an absolute age of 454 million years. In your own words, explain how scientists could estimate the ages of the other fossils in the diagram based on this information.

© Houghton Mifflin Harcourt

Geologic Timescale

Evidence from absolute dating indicates that Earth is about 4.5 billion years old. To help make sense of this vast amount of time, scientists use the geologic timescale to organize Earth's history. The geologic time scale divides Earth's history into intervals of time defined by major events or changes on Earth. The largest category of time is the eon, which is further divided into eras, periods, epochs, and ages.

Dividing that long period of time into smaller parts makes it easier for scientists to communicate their findings about rocks and fossils.

The Geologic Timescale

Unlike divisions of time such as days or minutes, the divisions of the geologic timescale are based on events in Earth's geologic history. Some divisions are based on the fossil record.

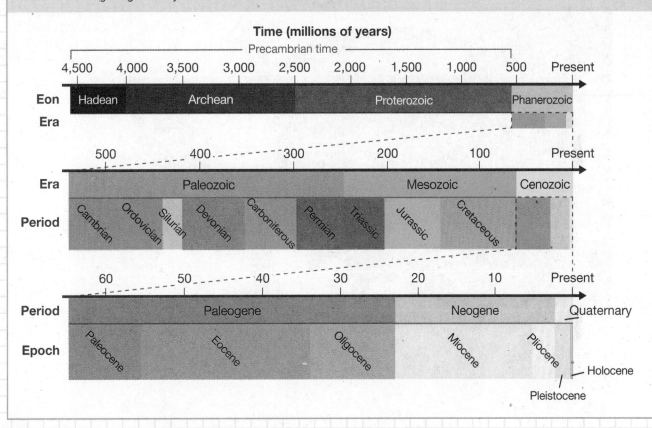

Do the Math | Using Models The geologic time of Earth spans more than 4.5 billion years. Let a football field, which is 100 yards long, model the number of years since Earth formed about 4,500,000,000 years ago.

14. Using this data, how many years of Earth's history would each yard line on the football field represent?

15. The first modern humans appeared on Earth about 200,000 years ago. Would it be possible to measure that number in terms of feet on a football field? Explain your answer.

© Houghton Mifflin Harcourt

16. *Dorudon* whales lived during the late Eocene Epoch. Where does that fall on the geologic timescale? How might the time at which the whale was alive have been determined? Record your evidence.

Estimate the Age of a Fossil

Suppose you found this turtle fossil in a layer of sedimentary rock. You observe that the rock layer also includes many tiny, fossilized, plate-like structures called *coccoliths*. These tiny plates once protected marine algae called *coccolithophores*. You find out that coccolith fossils are good index fossils.

This fossilized sea turtle has bite marks in its shell, indicating that it was in a predator-prey relationship with another creature.

These coccoliths are index fossils.

17. Which methods could you use to help estimate the age of the turtle fossil? Select all that apply.

    A. date the fossil with a radiometric dating method

    B. date the fossil with a relative dating method

    C. look up the age of the coccolith index fossil

    D. date a nearby igneous rock layer with a radiometric dating method

© Houghton Mifflin Harcourt • Image Credits: (t) ©Corbin17/Alamy; (b) ©Biophoto Associates/Science Source

Analyzing Fossil Data

Scientists have gathered a lot of data about fossils. When scientists organize, analyze, and interpret the data, they observe patterns. These patterns provide information about the types of organisms that have lived on Earth. A fossil can provide information about where the organism lived, the type of environment it lived in, and what it looked like. Scientists may also be able to infer how a species moved, whether it lived alone or in groups, what it ate, and whether it raised its young.

18. What types of data might a scientist get from studying coprolites?

Coprolites, or "dung stones," are fossilized animal wastes. They may include bones, scales, and plant parts that were not completely digested.

The Fossil Record

The collection of all known fossils and their placement in order from earliest to most recent is known as the **fossil record**. Therefore, the fossil record is the history of life on Earth as it is preserved by fossils. Scientists continue to revise their understanding of the fossil record as they find new information. However, the fossil record has limitations. Not all organisms that have lived on Earth are represented in the record. Many species left no fossils, or Earth processes destroyed their fossil remains.

While the fossil record does not contain fossils of all organisms that ever lived, it does provide evidence that life on Earth has been very diverse and has changed over time. Scientists have discovered that some organisms in the fossil record are similar to living organisms today, while others are quite different. For example, we know about trilobites from fossils, but no trilobites are alive today.

Patterns in the Fossil Record

Some large-scale patterns can be observed in the fossil record. For example, 95% of all discovered fossils are marine organisms, mostly shellfish. Only 0.012% of discovered fossils are vertebrates. So, the fossil record of marine organisms is far more complete than that of land animals or plants.

Scientists also observe that some fossils are complete skeletons or remains of organisms. Other fossils show only parts of organisms. Complete fossils are rare because the remains of dead organisms are usually eaten or scattered by predators and scavengers. The remains of organisms that died in water were most likely scattered in the direction of the water flow.

Another pattern in the fossil record is that the older the fossil, the more different its body structure is compared to current living organisms. Also, there are many instances where a species disappears from the fossil record, never to reappear. These species are said to be extinct. **Extinction** is when all members of a species die out.

© Houghton Mifflin Harcourt • Image Credits: ©wwing/E+/Getty Images

Mass Extinctions

Scientists have identified at least five major mass extinctions in Earth's history. During a *mass extinction*, large numbers of species die on different parts of Earth during a relatively short period of time. Scientists identify a mass extinction in the past by the disappearance of many species from the fossil record. The vast majority of all organisms that ever lived on Earth are extinct.

Scientists are not certain what caused these mass extinctions. They think, however, that the extinctions may have resulted from global events such volcanic eruptions, climate warming or cooling, or meteorite impacts on Earth's surface.

19. Scientists found many different types of fossils in a rock layer, which was dated at 251–299 million years old using an index fossil. In layers directly above that point, scientists found a large decrease in the number of fossils, particularly of marine and insect fossils. When did the extinction event occur?

Physical Evidence of Anatomy and Behavior

One reason that scientists have been able to gather so much information about Earth's past is because different kinds of fossils provide different information. Consider the information that can be gathered from trace fossils. Trace fossils are evidence of an organism's activity. They include clues such as footprints, tooth marks, tracks, scratches, burrows, coprolites, and nests. From trace fossils, scientists can figure out how much an organism weighed, how fast it moved, how it moved, and what it ate.

For example, footprints provide evidence of how many toes an animal had and whether the animal walked on two feet or four feet. By measuring the size and depth of the footprint and how far apart the footprints are, scientists can determine how fast it was moving, how tall it was, and how much it weighed.

The size and depth of the footprint from this three-toed dinosaur indicates that it was much larger than a human.

 EVIDENCE NOTEBOOK

20. What kinds of inferences might be made about the extinct whale's behavior based on its fossils? Record your evidence.

© Houghton Mifflin Harcourt • Image Credits: (t) ©Dragos Cosmin photos/Moment Open/ Getty Images; (b) ©FLPA/Alamy

Do the Math

Use Trace Fossils to Describe an Extinct Organism's Behavior

The actual size of an extinct organism is most accurately estimated from fossils. However, scientists can infer the size, activity, and speed of movement of an extinct organism from its footprint tracks. Analyzing trace fossils like this can also help determine if an extinct species lived in groups or was solitary.

21. Complete the following steps to find hip height, stride length, and whether the dinosaur was walking or running.

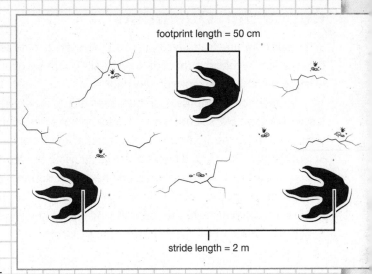

footprint length = 50 cm

stride length = 2 m

STEP 1 The length of a dinosaur footprint (f) is the distance from the back of its foot to the very top of the print. Scientists have identified mathematical relationships between the footprint length, hip height, and length of bipedal (two-legged) dinosaurs. The hip height is four times the foot length (a ratio of 4:1). Therefore, multiply the length of the footprint by 4 to find the hip height of the animal.

$f \times 4$ = hip height

STEP 2 To identify whether the dinosaur was running or walking, measure the stride length of the prints. This is the distance from one footprint to the next footprint made by the same foot. In this example, the stride length is 2 meters.

STEP 3 The ratio relationship between the hip height and stride length identifies whether the dinosaur was running or walking. (Remember to use the same units of length in your calculations.)

$$\frac{\text{stride length}}{\text{hip height}} = \text{ratio}$$

A ratio of 2.0 or less indicates the dinosaur was walking.
A ratio of 2.0 to 1:2.9 indicates the dinosaur was trotting.
A ratio of 2.9 or greater indicates the dinosaur was running.

22. What can you tell about the ratio relationship between stride length of the tracks and the hip height? Why would a longer stride length indicate a faster stride?

© Houghton Mifflin Harcourt

23. Engineer It Suppose you are on a class field trip to collect fossil shark teeth from a sandy beach. Which of the following tools would be the best for your teacher to take along for you to use to collect the shark's teeth? Choose all that apply.

A. mobile x-ray machine (uses x-rays to "see" inside things)

B. hand trowel (a small shovel with a pointed tip)

C. hand sieve (separates particles of different sizes)

D. power drill (hand-held tool that drills holes in things)

Sharks have few hard tissues, so teeth are often the only part that becomes fossilized.

Remaining Questions

Scientists continue to study fossils, and their efforts have led to many new and exciting discoveries. As the amount of data on fossils builds up over time, scientists can use existing data to make sense of new data.

As technology improves, so does the ability of scientists to gather information from fossils. For example, scientists now use scanning technologies to look inside fossils. These techniques have resulted in three-dimensional images of fossils and their structures. Scientists have even found traces of actual dinosaur tissues that never fossilized.

As new fossils are discovered and new information is gained, scientists revise the fossil record. Because not all environments were good for preserving remains as fossils, the fossil record will never be complete. Scientists continue to study the old fossils and newly discovered ones to gain more information about the history of life on Earth.

Interpret Fossils of Living Species

Not every fossil in the fossil record is of an extinct species. Some plant and animal species found in the fossil record are alive today and have changed relatively little over millions of years. The horseshoe crab is one example. Fossil evidence indicates that horseshoe crabs have lived on Earth for almost 450 million years. So, by the time dinosaurs appeared on Earth, horseshoe crabs had been around for 220 million years! Horseshoe crabs live in shallow marine environments. They are more closely related to spiders than they are to crabs.

A living horseshoe crab is next to a mold of an ancient horseshoe crab. Horseshoe crabs are called "living fossils" because their bodies have changed very little over time.

24. Compare the horseshoe crab that lives today with the fossil that is millions of years old. What kind of habitat do you think its fossilized ancestor lived in? Explain your answer.

_____

_____

_____

_____

© Houghton Mifflin Harcourt • Image Credits: ©Jeffrey L. Rotman/Corbis Documentary/ Getty Images

Continue You Exploration

Name: _____   Date: _____

Check out the path below or go online to choose one of the other paths shown.

People in Science

- **Hands-On Labs** 🖐
- **Comparing Similarities and Differences between Fossils**
- **Propose Your Own Path**

Go online to choose one of these other paths.

Nicholas Steno, Anatomist and Geologist

Nicholas Steno (1638–1686) was a Catholic bishop whose scientific studies focused on anatomy. In 1666, a shark was caught off the coast of Italy, and its head was sent to Steno to dissect. While studying the shark, he realized that the shark's teeth looked exactly like the unusual stony objects called *tongue stones* that were found in the countryside. Tongue stones had been a mystery for a long time. Steno showed that tongue stones and sharks' teeth were the same thing.

At the time, fossils were thought to either grow within the rocks in which they were found or fall to Earth from the moon. Steno used scientific reasoning to identify that fossils did not grow within rocks. He proposed that they were laid within a free-flowing substance that later hardened around the solid object. He used similar deductive reasoning to determine that younger layers of rock would be on top of older layers of rock.

Steno's career in science did not last long, but his work on the formation of rock strata and fossils was very important in the development of modern geology.

© Houghton Mifflin Harcourt • Image Credits: (t) ©SPL/Science Source; (b) ©Paul D. Stewart/Science Source

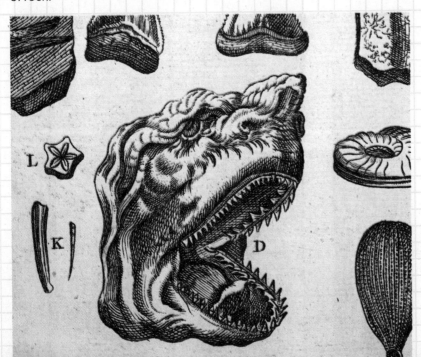

Steno dissected a shark and then created a book titled *Head of a Shark Dissected*, in which he included these sketches and diagrams.

Continue You Exploration

1. How would you explain to Steno how fossil shark teeth could be found in the countryside?

These fossilized shark teeth are just a few of the types that can be found today.

2. In your own words, how do you think Steno would have described the way horizontal layers of rock form?

3. Based on what you know about fossil formation, what do you think is the "free-flowing substance" Steno talked about?

4. **Collaborate** As a group, research the types of data Steno used to come to the conclusion that tongue stones were very old and were ancient sharks' teeth. What evidence and reasoning led to his conclusions? Present your findings to the class.

© Houghton Mifflin Harcourt • Image Credits: ©cordimages/iStock/Getty Images Plus/ Getty Images

Can You Explain It?

Name: _____   **Date:** _____

How can fossils help us learn about a whale that lived 40 million years ago?

© Houghton Mifflin Harcourt • Image Credits: ©A&E Television Networks/The Image Bank/ Getty Images

Explore
ONLINE!

EVIDENCE NOTEBOOK

Refer to the notes in your Evidence Notebook to help you construct an explanation for how fossils can help us learn about the extinct whale.

1. State your claim. Make sure your claim fully explains what we can tell about extinct organisms from their fossils.

2. Summarize the evidence you have gathered to support your claim and explain your reasoning.

Checkpoints

Answer the following questions to check your understanding of the lesson.

Use the photo of the carbonized fossil to answer Question 3.

3. Which statement describes the types of data scientists can obtain directly from observing this fossil?

   A. the exact time the organism lived

   B. the color of the living organism

   C. where the organism lived

   D. the physical structures of the organism

Use the photo of the Grand Canyon to answer Questions 4 and 5.

4. This photo shows layers of
   sedimentary rock / fossils.
   The oldest layers were laid down
   first / most recently and therefore
   are closest to the surface / bottom.

5. Assuming that each rock layers formed horizontally, which layer is the oldest?

   A. layer A

   B. layer B

   C. layer C

   D. layer D

6. A scientist compares a fossil to a very similar living organism. What might the scientist be able to infer based on this comparison? Select all that apply.

   A. Absolute age of the fossil

   B. When the fossil organism likely lived

   C. What the fossil organism likely ate

   D. Environment the fossil organism likely lived in

© Houghton Mifflin Harcourt • Image Credits: (t) ©DEA/G. CIGOLINI/De Agostini/Getty Images; (b) ©markhiggins/iStock/Getty Images Plus/Getty Images

Interactive Review

Complete this section to review the main concepts of the lesson.

Fossils form in many different ways. Not all organisms form fossils when they die because conditions must be just right for a fossil to form.

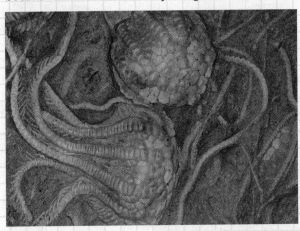

A. Explain why most organisms that have lived on Earth do not form fossils.

The relative age of a rock layer describes whether it is older or younger than another layer. The absolute age of a rock layer is its actual age in years.

B. How do scientists use relative and absolute ages of rock layers to estimate the ages of fossils?

The fossil record is the history of life on Earth as it is preserved by fossils.

C. What kind of information can scientists learn from different types of fossils?

© Houghton Mifflin Harcourt • Image Credits: (t) ©Kevin Schafer/Alamy Images; (b) ©wwing/E+/Getty Images

Patterns of Change in Life on Earth

Titanis walleri, or Waller's terror bird, was flightless. It could grow up to 1.8 m (5.9 feet) tall, about the same height as an adult human. It lived from about 2 to 5 million years ago.

By the end of this lesson . . .

you will be able to analyze patterns in the fossil record to explain how life changed over time.

© Houghton Mifflin Harcourt • Image Credits: ©Aunt_Spray/iStock/Getty Images Plus/Getty Images

Go online to view the digital version of the Hands-On Lab for this lesson and to download additional lab resources.

CAN YOU EXPLAIN IT?

What can explain the formation of a rock layer with no fossils in between rock layers with different types of fossils?

fossils found

no fossils found

fossils found

Major changes to populations of organisms and environments happened in the past. Such events from the past are recorded in rock layers as part of the fossil record.

1. What is needed for a fossil to form? Select all that apply.

   A. The organism must first get stuck in rock.

   B. The soft tissue of the dead organism must be eaten by scavengers before the bones can be preserved.

   C. The tracks or burrows of an organism must be filled with sediments before they are disturbed.

   D. The organism's body must be covered by sediment or another substance before its body decays.

2. What are some reasons why a rock layer may not have any fossils?

EVIDENCE NOTEBOOK As you explore the lesson, gather evidence to help explain why a fossil-free rock layer might exist between layers with fossils.

© Houghton Mifflin Harcourt • Image Credits: ©Dr. Robert Spicer/Science Source

Analyzing Evidence About the History of Life

Only a small percentage of the organisms that ever lived fossilized. Yet, these fossils help scientists learn about how life on Earth changed over time. Fossils show where and when certain extinct organisms lived. They also show patterns in how the body plans of organisms changed over time. Fossils can provide information about past environments. They can even give clues to how extinct species interacted. The fossil record also shows patterns in how species appeared and disappeared throughout Earth's history.

Glyptodonts were about the size of a small car. They ate plants and lived among early humans before the Ice Age.

The insect-eating armadillo shares many features with its extinct relative, the glyptodont. However, it is much smaller.

3. Compare the armadillo to the glyptodont (GLIP•tuh•dahnt). What similarities provide evidence that they might be related?

Evidence of Earliest Life Forms

Charles Walcott was an American paleontologist who, in 1909, discovered many well-preserved fossils of ancient sea organisms near Mount Burgess, Canada. The fossils were preserved in layers of shale left by an ancient ocean. The soft tissues of many of the fossilized organisms in the Burgess Shale were preserved in great detail.

Scientists used a method of radiometric dating to find the absolute age of nearby igneous rock layers. These layers contain a type of potassium that changes into argon at a constant rate. Scientists measure how much potassium in the rock has changed to argon. From this measurement, they can determine when the igneous rock formed. After finding the age of the igneous rock, they used relative dating to determine that the Burgess Shale fossils are over 500 million years old. This seems quite old. But, the earliest evidence for life dates back about 3.8 *billion* years! The earliest organisms were single cells, which rarely formed fossils. Evidence of these earliest cells was found in rock samples with high levels of a type of carbon only found in living things.

© Houghton Mifflin Harcourt • Image Credits: (l) ©Roman Garcia Mora/Stocktrek Images/Getty Images; (r) ©saddako/iStock/Getty Images Plus/Getty Images

Traces of Carbon from Cells

There are different types of carbon atoms. But living organisms only use one of these types. Scientists detected high levels of this type of carbon in ancient rock compared to other types of carbon. They concluded that there was life on Earth at the time this ancient rock formed 3.8 billion years ago. Fossilized cells were not found in this rock, only chemical evidence of life. This is an example of *inference*, using evidence to draw conclusions when direct observation of a process or event is not possible. These rocks contain the earliest known evidence of life on Earth.

Many types of scientists work together to collect evidence of ancient life. Chemists isolate certain chemicals from rock samples to analyze them. Biologists study how living things use chemicals in their bodies. Geologists determine the age of rocks and what Earth conditions may have caused them to form. Paleontologists find and study fossils.

The ratio of different type of carbon in these 3.8 billion year-old rocks in Greenland is interpreted as evidence of life on Earth at the time the rocks formed.

Fossil Evidence

The earliest fossilized cells scientists have found are about 3.5 billion years old. The fossils are of a type of *cyanobacteria*, a single-celled life form that makes its own food by photosynthesis. In Greek, *cyano-* means "blue." The bacteria left traces of the blue-green pigment protein that gives them their name. The cyanobacteria also left behind stromatolite formations. *Stromatolites* are layered mounds, columns, or sheets of calcium-rich sedimentary rock. They are made of layers of bacteria and sediment.

Evidence of Ancient Cellular Life

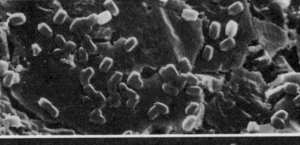

Ancient Cyanobacteria Fossils of bacteria similar to these were found in ancient stromatolites from western Australia. The stromatolites were about 3.5 billion years old. Cyanobacteria are a type of bacteria that capture the energy of sunlight and release oxygen during photosynthesis. They helped create an oxygen-rich atmosphere on ancient Earth.

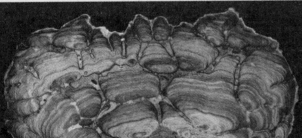

Stromatolite Growth Patterns Notice the light and dark layers of this stromatolite. They are caused by the growth patterns of cyanobacteria that were on Earth when each layer was formed. The bacteria release white-colored calcium compounds that mix with soil or sand deposits. Over time, the layers harden into rock.

Modern Stromatolites These stromatolites line the sea floor of Shark Bay in western Australia. They are usually columns or domes because the cyanobacteria that form them group together in mat-like sheets. New groups form mats on top of the sediment deposits trapped by older groups.

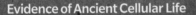

© Houghton Mifflin Harcourt • Image Credits: (t) ©James L. Amos/Corbis Documentary/Getty Images; (tc) ©Philippe Plailly/Science Source; (bc) ©Ted Kinsman/Science Source; (b) ©Michael Aw/Lonely Planet Images/Getty Images

4. Do the Math Scientists estimate that Earth is 4.54 billion years old. Chemical evidence of life appears in the fossil record 3.8 billion years ago. What percentage of Earth's history was without life? Write a formula for the calculation using variables you define. Then use your formula to find the answer.

5. Think about the process of identifying the age of the earliest fossils. How does it show how scientists use evidence and logic to answer scientific questions?

Evidence of Change Over Time

For more than 2 billion years, only single-celled life existed on Earth. That changed about 540 million years ago, during the Cambrian Era. Scientists found a large increase in the number and types of fossils in rock layers that formed during this time. Cambrian organisms looked very different from living things today. Many Cambrian species, such as *Marrella*, were arthropods. *Arthropods* are a group of invertebrate animals that have segmented bodies. Cambrian arthropods are now extinct. But arthropods such as ants and lobsters are alive today. Scientists observe a large increase in the variety of fossils formed during this time, so this time is often called the *Cambrian explosion*.

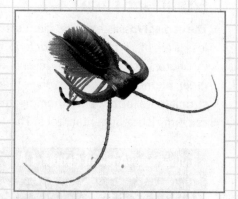

Marrella is the most common fossil found in Burgess Shale.

Many scientists think the Cambrian explosion happened because of increased oxygen levels in the air from cyanobacteria and new interactions among organisms. The fossil record shows that many Cambrian animals had hard outer shells. These shells could protect the animals from predators. Scientists infer that the rise of the first predators on Earth led to a greater diversity of life forms. Over many generations, populations developed a variety of behaviors and characteristics, such as hard outer shells, in response to the action of predators. The fossil record of the Cambrian explosion gives scientists a way to investigate how life changes over time.

6. What evidence from the fossil record supports the observation that life changes over time? Select all that apply.

   A. more fossils of the same species found in several rock layers

   B. increased numbers of fossils of different species found in younger rock layers

   C. several rock layers that do not contain fossils

   D. fossils of distant relatives of a modern species found in ancient rock layers

EVIDENCE NOTEBOOK

   7. What does a rock layer with very few fossils suggest about conditions in that region when the rock layer formed? Record your evidence.

© Houghton Mifflin Harcourt • Image Credits: ©Chase Studio/Science Source

Increasing Complexity of Fossils

Scientists find that more recent rock layers contain fossils that have more complex bodies and physical features than earlier fossils. Multicellular organisms first appeared in the fossil record more than 600 million years ago (mya). Jawless fish appeared in the fossil record about 500 mya. Fish with jaws appeared nearly 400 mya. Later rock layers include amphibians and then reptiles and mammals. Birds appeared more recently. This evidence suggests that new physical features, such as feet and lungs, enabled organisms to live in new habitats. Once living in these new habitats, populations became more different from each other over many generations.

The fossils of organisms with simpler body plans are also found in younger rock layers along with more complex fossils. Scientists infer that while life changes over time on Earth, not all populations change at the same rate. For example, there is no evidence that modern bacteria are any more complex than bacteria found in ancient rock layers.

The Increase in the Complexity of Life on Earth Over Time

Scientists use fossil evidence to determine the periods of major changes in the body plans of organisms. They also use this evidence to infer likely causes for the changes.

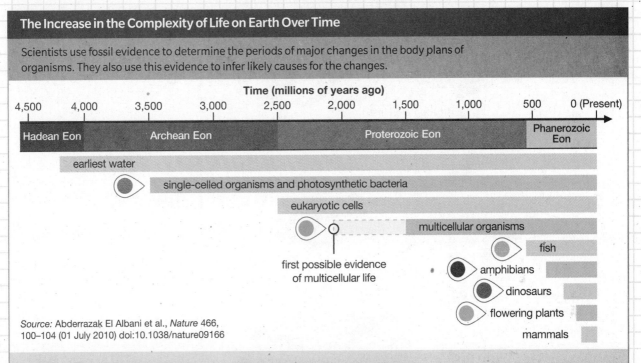

Source: Abderrazak El Albani et al., *Nature* 466, 100–104 (01 July 2010) doi:10.1038/nature09166

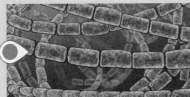

The earliest life forms were single cells. These cells could perform only the most basic life functions.

The *Dickinsonia* genus included some of the first complex multicellular organisms, which lived about 600 mya.

Metaspriggina, a genus of the earliest fish, lived about 505 mya. They had gills, worm-like bodies, and large eyes.

Members of the *Cacops* genus lived about 280 mya. They evolved from fish with bony fins and lung-like organs.

The *Captorhinus* genus, the first reptiles to live on land, date back to 300 mya. They were similar to lizards.

Seed plants of the *Archaeosperma* genus lived about 375 mya. They gave rise to flowering plants 160 mya.

© Houghton Mifflin Harcourt

Transitional Fossils

Using evidence from the fossil record, scientists conclude that life began in the oceans. Early fish-like organisms gave rise to fish, which gave rise to the ancestor common to amphibians. To determine how changes like these occur in nature, scientists look for *transitional fossils*. These are fossils of organisms that have body structures that are found both in an ancestral species and in its descendants. For example, when scientists investigated the origins of amphibians, they hypothesized that there might have been an organism that had traits of both fish and amphibians. This hypothesis was supported with the discovery of a fossil, called *Tiktaalik*. *Tiktaalik* lived in the water. It had bones in its fins that were very similar to the wrist and feet bones of amphibians.

Fossil Evidence of the Transition from Ocean to Land

The fossil of *Tiktaalik* is a transitional fossil in the evolution of amphibians from their fish ancestors. It has both fish and amphibian characteristics.

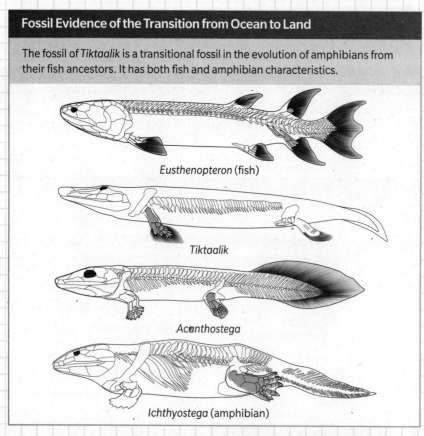

Eusthenopteron (fish)

Tiktaalik

Acanthostega

Ichthyostega (amphibian)

8. At some point in the past, the bones in the fins of a population of fish became larger and longer. The bones became able to support the weight of the organisms when they were out of water. This happened over many generations. What other changes over time would be needed for fish to live out of the water?

9. Biological structures often have shapes (form) that enable organisms to perform particular tasks (function). How do transitional fossils, such as *Tiktaalik*, show that form is connected to function in living things?

© Houghton Mifflin Harcourt

Infer How Features Changed Over Time

Whales swim and live in the ocean. Yet, they are mammals. They have traits similar to those of mammals that live on land. They give birth to live young, feed their young with milk, and have hair. Evidence from the fossil record supports the theory that the ancestors of whales lived on land before they moved into water. Over time, several body structures, such as the skull, hips, and legs, changed. These changes made the structures better adapted to swimming than walking.

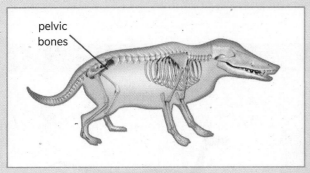

Pakicetus inachus lived around 50 million years ago.

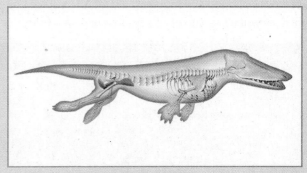

Ambulocetus natans lived 50–45 million years ago.

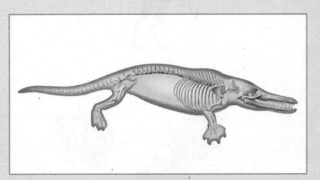

Kutchicetus minimus lived 46–43 million years ago.

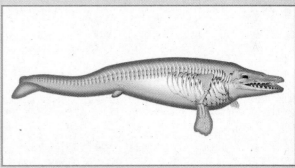

Dorudon atrox lived 40–34 million years ago.

10. Hind legs are connected to pelvic bones, which are important for walking. Modern whales have relatively small pelvic bones. How did the pelvic bones of whales' ancestors change over time?

_____

_____

_____

_____

_____

_____

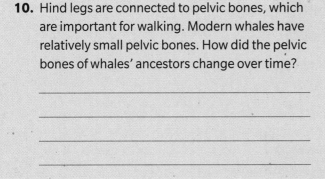

The modern bowhead whale is a living species that has been on Earth for 35 million years.

11. The form of a body structure is related to its function. Given this, how can you tell that Pakicetus inachus most likely lived on land and that Dorudon atrox lived in water?

_____

_____

_____

_____

© Houghton Mifflin Harcourt

Analyzing Patterns in the Number of Life Forms Over Time

The fossil record shows changes in species and increases in biodiversity over time. It also shows the loss of certain species over time. When a species dies out, its fossils no longer occur in the fossil record. Scientists observe that the loss of species from the fossil record seems to happen at a regular rate. Yet, there have been time periods during Earth's history when the rate of species loss was very high.

Identifying Extinction Events in the Fossil Record

Geologic time periods are identified by major changes in the fossil record. The side of this cliff in Palo Duro Canyon State Park in Texas includes the Permian-Triassic (P-T) extinction boundary. The P-T mass extinction happened about 248 million years ago.

Coelophysis fossils appear after the P-T extinction. They were a genus of small, meat-eating dinosaurs.

Trilobite fossils are found in the fossil record before the P-T extinction. They are not found afterward.

12. Explain one inference you can make about fossils from the information in the rock layer images.

Extinction

An **extinction** occurs when a species dies out and there are no members of the species left on Earth. The fossil record shows an extinction when a species is no longer found in sedimentary rock layers. For example, trilobites were once very common marine arthropods. They disappeared from the fossil record after the Permian-Triassic extinction, which indicates that trilobites became extinct.

A *mass extinction* happens when whole groups of related species die out at about the same time. Mass extinctions appear to be caused by large changes to the environment. When so many organisms die, there are many new opportunities for surviving species to use ecosystem resources. They then thrive and change over time. The numbers of new species found in the fossil record after each mass extinction eventually increases over time.

© Houghton Mifflin Harcourt • Image Credits: ©mtcurado/istock/Getty Images Plus/ Getty Images

The Five Mass Extinction Events on Earth			
Extinction event	Proposed cause	Organisms affected	An organism that went extinct
Ordovician-Silurian, 443 million years ago	Rapid shifts in tectonic plates; climate change, which lead to the formation of glaciers that caused sea levels to drop	Up to 85% of all species; 45%–60% of families of marine organisms died out	*Orthoceras*
Late Devonian, 354 million years ago	Possibly a large comet strike; possible decrease in global temperatures due to dust and debris from comet strike; drop in sea levels	70%–80% of all species; marine life affected more than freshwater and land organisms	*Dunkleosteus*
Permian-Triassic, 248 million years ago	Volcanic eruptions, release of methane from the sea floor; low oxygen levels in oceans, drop in sea levels	Largest extinction; about 80%–85% of all marine and land vertebrate species died out, including all trilobites and many insect species	*Dimetrodon*
Triassic-Jurassic, 200 million years ago	Poorly understood; possibly an extreme decrease in sea level and lower oxygen levels in oceans	About 50% of all species disappeared; end of mammal-like reptiles, leaving mainly dinosaurs	*Typothorax*
Cretaceous-Tertiary, 65 million years ago	Volcanic eruptions and climate cooling; drop in sea levels; large asteroid or comet strike	47% of marine life and 18% of land vertebrates died, including non-avian dinosaurs; mainly turtles, small reptiles, birds, and mammals left	*Quetzalcoatlus*

13. Mass extinctions are caused by global / regional environmental changes. During a mass extinction event, biodiversity in the fossil record increases / decreases.

© Houghton Mifflin Harcourt

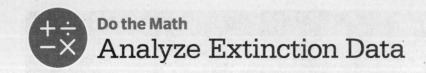

Do the Math
Analyze Extinction Data

Scientists compare rock layers before and after a mass extinction to estimate the number of affected species. They make estimates from several rock layer samples. Then they compare the loss of species to the normal rate of extinction that happens as life changes over time. This allows scientists to estimate the percentage of species on Earth affected by a mass extinction. The number of extinctions over time can be graphed. These graphs show a relatively constant extinction rate, broken up by large changes in the number of families of organisms lost during mass extinction events.

14. Describe the trends you see in each graph. What is the relationship between mass extinctions and biodiversity over time?

15. Does the top graph provide evidence that extinctions are a normal part of Earth's history? Explain your reasoning.

16. Mass extinctions do / do not cause permanent reductions in biodiversity on Earth. After each extinction event, the number of families increases / decreases rapidly over time.

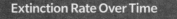

Extinction Rate Over Time

The fossil record shows five mass extinctions. During each one, more than half of Earth's species went extinct.

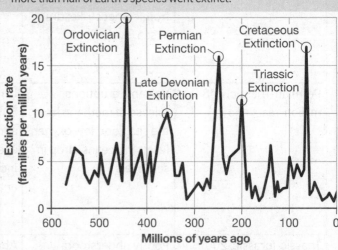

Source: Adapted from Howard Hughes Medical Center. HHMI Mass Extinctions Interactive and University of California Museum of Paleontology's Understanding Evolution. Accessed on September 22, 2016.

Diversity of Marine Organisms Over Time

Each mass extinction greatly reduced biodiversity. Yet, the species that remained expanded and diverged over time.

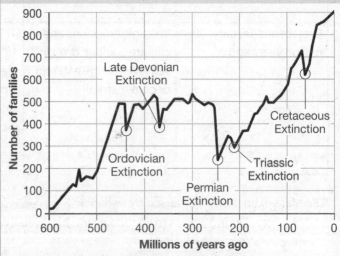

Source: Sepkoski J.J. Jr, 1984, "A kinetic model of Phanerozoic taxonomic diversity, III. Post Paleozoic families and mass extinctions" Paleobiology 10: 246-267. Accessed on September 25, 2016.

© Houghton Mifflin Harcourt

Patterns in Extinction and Biodiversity Data

Scientists want to find the causes of mass extinctions. To do this, they analyze rock layers before, during, and after an extinction event. For example, when studying the Cretaceous-Paleogene, or K-Pg, mass extinction, they looked at the rock layers laid down at the beginning of this extinction. They discovered unusual amounts of a metal called *iridium* in one rock layer in many different places of Earth. Iridium is rare on Earth. But it is common in asteroids. They also discovered tiny glass formations

The *Alphadon* was a small mammal that survived the K-Pg extinction. It likely did so by burrowing underground to avoid the dangerous conditions.

that are often found near craters caused by meteorite impacts. The high temperature caused by the impact melts sand. Glass spheres and other shapes form from the melted sand. Scientists used this evidence to infer that a very large meteorite struck Earth. It caused large-scale changes to Earth's environment. Large animal species were affected the most. Nearly all dinosaurs disappeared from the fossil record at this time. Fossil evidence shows that small mammals that could burrow to avoid the hot temperatures that resulted from the impact survived. It also shows that surviving species spread and diversified. Mass extinctions such as this are followed by periods of rapid growth in Earth's biodiversity.

17. Observe the patterns in plant diversity shown in the graph. How might species of flowering plants have survived the K-Pg extinction?

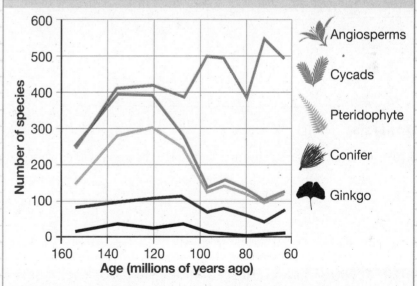

Plant Diversification Over Time

Mass extinctions also affect plant species. Some plant families decline after extinction events. Other plant families increase in number afterward. Angiosperms, or flowering plants, are a family that diversified over time.

Angiosperms
Cycads
Pteridophyte
Conifer
Ginkgo

Primary Source: JC McElwain, KJ Willis, and R Lupia's chapter: "Cretaceous CO_2 decline and the Radiation and Diversification of Angiosperms," as quoted by *A History of Atmospheric CO_2 and its effects on Plants, Animals and Ecosystems* by TE Cerling and MD Dearing, page 135. Accessed on January 11, 2017.

© Houghton Mifflin Harcourt • Image Credits: ©Dorling Kindersley/Getty Images

Hands-On Lab
Model Analysis of the Fossil Record

You will analyze fossil data to identify evidence of extinction and the appearance of new species over time

Scientists compare fossil evidence from different places on Earth. They observe certain fossil types in the same rock layers across multiple locations. In some layers, they observe the disappearance of certain fossil types. In some layers, they observe the appearance of new fossil types. By determining the relative age of rock layers that contain fossils, scientists can identify these patterns of appearance and disappearance in the fossil record.

MATERIALS
- colored pencils
- scissors

Procedure

STEP 1 On a separate sheet of paper, copy the *Sedimentary Rock Layers from Four Locations* shown on the next page. Be sure to include the symbols that represent different types of fossils. Cut out the rock sequence from each location. Then line them up so that rock layers with similar compositions are side by side.

STEP 2 Analyze the fossil types found in different layers. Identify the species that appear to have gone extinct based on these fossil data.

STEP 3 Complete the table by drawing the symbols of three different fossils.

Fossil from oldest layer	Fossil from youngest layer	Fossil species that goes extinct

Analysis

STEP 4 What patterns in the rock layer fossils helped you identify an extinction?

STEP 5 Why is it necessary to see a similar pattern of change in fossils from several places in order to conclude that an extinction happened?

© Houghton Mifflin Harcourt

STEP 6 Analyze the fossil types found in the youngest rock layer. Which of these fossil species appeared first in the fossil record? Which one appeared more recently? How do you know?

Sedimentary Rock Layers from Four Locations

The different colors represent different types of sedimentary rock. The symbols within the rock layers represent different types of fossils

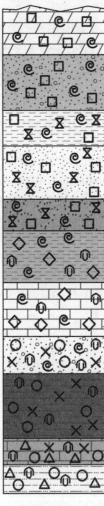
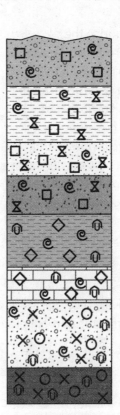
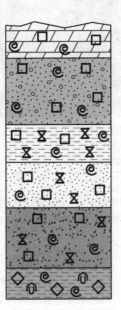
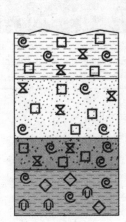

| Location 1 | Location 2 | Location 3 | Location 4 |

© Houghton Mifflin Harcourt

EVIDENCE NOTEBOOK

18. Why might different types of fossils be found in rock layers that come before and after a rock layer that contains no fossils? Record your evidence.

19. Engineer It Computed tomography (CT) scanners can give information about the inside of fragile bones, such as the skull of an early human ancestor. The CT images are a series of x-ray images that can be "stacked" to form a 3D virtual model. These virtual models can then be used to make physical 3D models of either the fossils or what was inside them. How can CT scanners solve the problem of damaging delicate fossils?

Language SmArts

Explain Inferences from Fossil Record Evidence

Ancient insects grew very large during the Carboniferous Period, about 320 million years ago. Scientists believe this was due in part to air that was high in oxygen. *Meganeura* was an ancestor of dragonflies. It had a wingspan over two feet wide!

Scientists have found thick coal deposits in Carboniferous rocks near *Meganeura* fossils. Coal deposits form from large amounts of decaying plant material. Such large amounts of plant material generally require warm and wet conditions.

Meganeura used its spiny legs to catch insects, lizards, and mammals living near ponds. Scientists think that insects grew so large because of the high oxygen levels in the air.

20. What modern organisms have an ecological role around ponds today that is similar to the role of *Meganeura* during the Carboniferous Period? Explain your answer.

_____

_____

_____

21. Write a series of logical steps that you could use to infer the type of climate that existed during *Meganeura's* time.

_____

_____

_____

_____

© Houghton Mifflin Harcourt • Image Credits: ©Mark Garlick/Science Photo Library/Getty Images

Continue Your Exploration

Name: _____ Date: _____

Check out the path below or go online to choose one of the other paths shown.

Prediction of a Transitional Fossil

- **Hands-On Labs** ✋
- **Reconstruct the Past from Physical Evidence**
- **Propose Your Own Path**

Go online to choose one of these other paths.

Transitional fossils are an important part of the fossil record. But how do scientists know how to spot a transitional fossil? They make hypotheses about the types of organisms that may have descended from earlier organisms and given rise to more recent organisms.

Scientists studied both ancient fish and amphibian fossils. They then predicted that an organism that shared some features in common with both fish and amphibian families likely lived in the past. They identified certain features that the hypothetical species—a "fishapod"—might have, such as a fish with feet. Their predictions were confirmed when fossils of the "fishapod" *Tiktaalik roseae* were found. The fossils showed that *Tiktaalik* had a skull and ribs like land animals. It also had several fish features, including fins and scales.

Tiktaalik roseae was found in the Canadian Arctic. Scientists found the front end of *Tiktaalik* 10 years before finding the hind end in different rock.

© Houghton Mifflin Harcourt • Image Credits: ©John Weinstein/Field Museum Library/ Getty Images

Continue Your Exploration

1. In order for *Tiktaalik* to be considered a transitional fossil, when does it need to have appeared in the fossil record?

   A. before fish and amphibians

   B. after amphibians

   C. at the same time as amphibians

   D. between fish and amphibians

2. It took more than 3 billion years for life to spread from the oceans onto land. All organisms that lived on land evolved during the 550 million years that followed. How might this relatively rapid diversification of land species be explained?

   A. The move to land environments led to more changes in species over time.

   B. The move to land environments led to fewer changes in species over time.

   C. Spreading to land did not affect the amount of change in species over time.

   D. The change in environments resulted in lower biodiversity.

3. Draw a simple sketch of a transitional fossil that might link feathered, tree-climbing reptiles to early birds. Label the features that connect the fossil to the reptile and to the bird.

4. **Collaborate** Work with a small group to research another transitional fossil discovery. What evidence did scientists provide to support the identification of the transitional fossil? Present your findings to the class.

© Houghton Mifflin Harcourt

Can You Explain It?

Name: _____ **Date:** _____

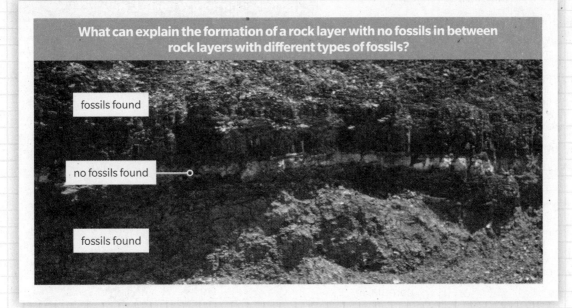

What can explain the formation of a rock layer with no fossils in between rock layers with different types of fossils?

fossils found

no fossils found

fossils found

EVIDENCE NOTEBOOK

Refer to the notes in your Evidence Notebook to help you construct an explanation for how a rock layer with no fossils might have formed between rock layers with different types of fossils.

1. State your claim. Make sure your claim fully explains how a rock layer with no fossils might have formed between rock layers with different types of fossils.

2. Summarize the evidence you have gathered to support your claim and explain your reasoning.

© Houghton Mifflin Harcourt • Image Credits: ©Dr. Robert Spicer/Science Source

Checkpoints

Answer the following questions to check your understanding of the lesson.

Use the diagram to answer Question 3.

3. How are the bones in the fin structure of the *Tiktaalik* evidence of a transition from fish to amphibian? Select all that apply.

   A. It has fins like a fish.

   B. It has limb bones like an amphibian.

   C. It is older than fish fossils.

   D. The limb bones do not look as developed as they do in the amphibian.

4. Organisms with more complex body plans are more likely to be found in older / younger rock layers. This observation supports the general pattern of increasing / decreasing complexity of physical structures in fossilized organisms.

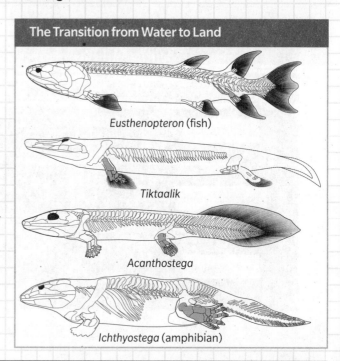

The Transition from Water to Land

Eusthenopteron (fish)

Tiktaalik

Acanthostega

Ichthyostega (amphibian)

Use the graph to answer Question 5.

5. Based on the graph, biodiversity increases / decreases during a mass extinction event and then increases / decreases after the event. In general, biodiversity on Earth increases / stays the same over time.

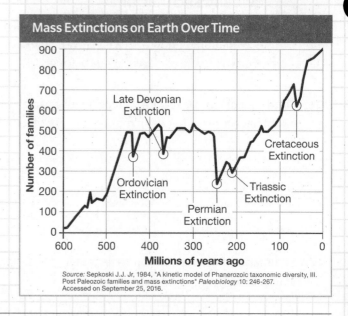

Mass Extinctions on Earth Over Time

Late Devonian Extinction

Ordovician Extinction

Permian Extinction

Triassic Extinction

Cretaceous Extinction

Number of families

Millions of years ago

Source: Sepkoski J.J. Jr, 1984, "A kinetic model of Phanerozoic taxonomic diversity, III. Post Paleozoic families and mass extinctions" *Paleobiology* 10: 246-267. Accessed on September 25, 2016.

© Houghton Mifflin Harcourt

6. What types of evidence allow scientists to infer that single-celled life likely existed 3.8 billion years ago? Select all that apply.

   A. transitional fossils in ancient rocks

   B. certain forms of carbon in ancient rock

   C. fossil evidence, such as stromatolites

   D. evidence of extinction events

Interactive Review

Complete this page to review the main concepts of the lesson.

Scientists use the fossil record to identify patterns of change in life on Earth. They use evidence to infer possible causes of the changes they observe.

A. What types of changes are recorded in the fossil record?

The fossil record provides evidence of five mass extinctions. Scientists compare fossils found in rock layers to find evidence about how organisms were affected by extinction events.

B. Draw a sketch of rock layers that includes evidence of an extinction. Use symbols to represent species that existed before, during, and after the extinction event.

© Houghton Mifflin Harcourt • Image Credits: ©Ted Kinsman/Science Source

Evidence of Common Ancestry

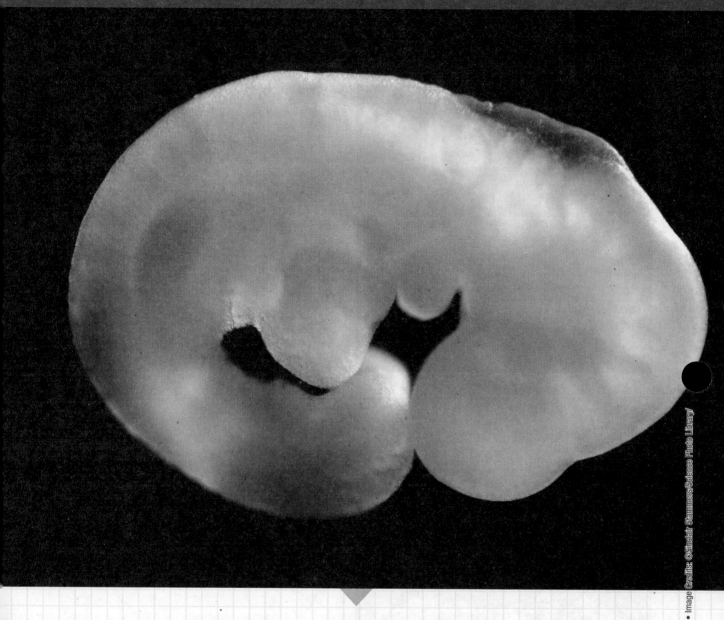

This is a 9.5 day-old mouse embryo. It has yet to grow organ systems, but it has a head, a tail, and tiny limb buds. Its heart is developing in the larger bulge below its head.

By the end of this lesson . . .

you will be able to analyze data to provide evidence for evolutionary relationships among organisms.

© Houghton Mifflin Harcourt • Image Credits: ©Sinclair Stammers/Science Photo Library/Getty Images

Go **online** to view the digital version of
the Hands-On Lab for this lesson and to
download additional lab resources.

CAN YOU EXPLAIN IT?

What evidence supports a relationship between extinct and modern birds?

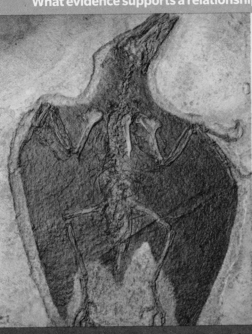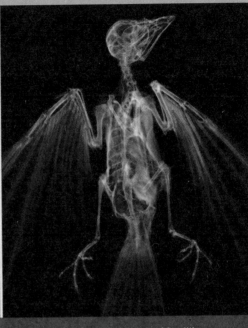

The fossil on the left is of an extinct bird genus called *Confuciusornis* that lived over 100 million years ago. The x-ray on the right shows the skeleton of a living crow species, *Corvus frugilegus*.

1. What similarities and differences can you observe from these photos?

2. Based on the fossil organism's body structures, how do you think it moved?

 EVIDENCE NOTEBOOK As you explore this lesson, gather evidence to help
explain the relationship between extinct and modern birds.

© Houghton Mifflin Harcourt • Image Credits: (l) ©Millard H. Sharp/Science Source; (r) ©D. Roberts/Science Source

Identifying Similarities Among Organisms

What would you think if you planted a sunflower seed and it grew into an oak tree? You would probably be very surprised! Of course, that would never actually happen. You know that sunflower seeds grow into sunflower plants. Oak tree seeds, or acorns, grow into oak trees. This is an example of a consistent and observable pattern in nature: Offspring look similar to their parents. A key assumption of science is the idea that natural systems have consistent, observable, and measurable patterns. These patterns and events happen in the same way today as they did in the past.

Explore ONLINE!

The baby elephant has a combination of genes from each parent. This is true of all offspring of living things that reproduce sexually. Because of this genetic recombination, the elephant will not be identical to either of its parents.

3. Would a baby elephant be more likely to look like its parent or to look like one of its great-great-great-grandparents? Explain your reasoning.

Living Organisms Reproduce and Pass on Traits

Organisms reproduce today just as they did in the past. In fact, organisms must reproduce or else life would no longer exist! We know that the offspring of sunflowers look similar to sunflowers, not oak trees. And the offspring of elephants look similar to elephants, not zebras. Offspring look similar to their parents because heritable traits are passed down from generation to generation. These heritable traits are encoded in genetic material called *DNA*. Genetic material is passed from generation to generation through the same processes today as it was in the past.

Evolution is the process of biological change by which populations become different from their ancestors over many generations. Differences develop in populations due to changes in the genetic material of individuals and the genetic make-up of populations. These changes build up over time, so the more recently two species shared a common ancestor, the more closely related those species are to each other. A **common ancestor** is an ancient species from which two or more species evolved.

© Houghton Mifflin Harcourt • Image Credits: ©john michael evan potter/Shutterstock

Evolution of Populations over Time

Whales and fish have similar body shapes. However, they are not closely related. Whales share a more recent common ancestor with land animals than they do with fish. In fact, whales' closest living relatives are hippos! Whales are very different from fish. They have lungs, nourish developing young inside the female's body, and produce milk. These characteristics are different from those of fish, but they are shared with mammals such as hippos.

Scientists learn about evolutionary relationships in many ways. They use a variety of evidence, including fossil evidence. They also analyze body structures and genetic evidence. All of these types of evidence support the hypothesis that modern whales evolved from hoofed mammals called *Anthracotheres* that lived on land.

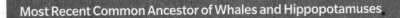

Most Recent Common Ancestor of Whales and Hippopotamuses

Anthracotheres lived around 50–60 million years ago. Over many millions of years, *Anthracotherium* populations evolved and developed into two main groups of organisms.

One group that is descended from Anthracotheres lived entirely in water. This group includes all species of whales and dolphins.

The other group lived mostly on land. Today, there are two species of hippos. They are the only remaining members of that group of land animals.

© Houghton Mifflin Harcourt • Image Credits: (r) ©EcoPrint/Shutterstock; (l) ©Brian J. Skerry/National Geographic/Getty Images

Evolution of Whales

The extinct species shown here are all ancient relatives of whales. The fossils of these extinct species have skeletal features that are similar to whales. Some features, such as the ear structure of the *Pakicetus*, are very similar to modern whales but unlike any other known mammal.

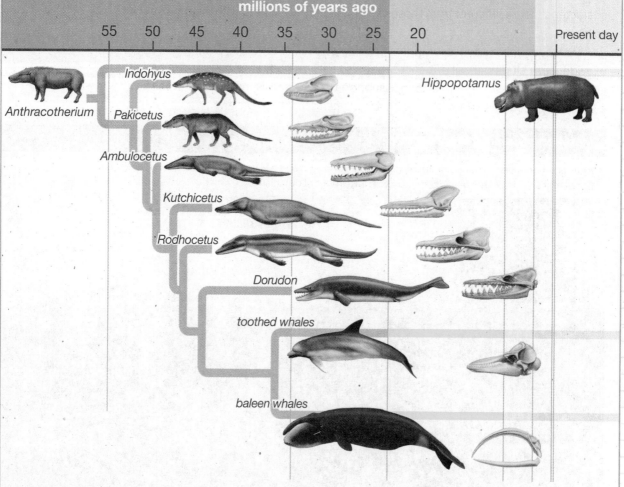

Source: University of California at Berkeley, Understanding Evolution, "The evolution of whales," accessed March 21, 2017; University of Wisconsin-Madison, The Paleobiology Database, 2015–2016; Mette E. Steeman et al., *Systematic Biology*, 2009 58 (6) 573–585

4. Genetic information, in the form of DNA / fossils, gets passed from generation to generation. Because of this, offspring look similar to / very unlike their parents. Over time, genetic changes add up. Populations come to look more and more similar to / different from their ancestors. For whales, this explains why Pakicetus / Rodhocetus looks the most different from modern whales. It looks most different because it is a very ancient / recent relative of whales.

5. Which conclusion can be made from the diagram of whale evolution?

   A. All known whale ancestors had four legs.

   B. Whale ancestors transitioned from land to water habitats.

   C. Only skulls show evidence of relationships among whale ancestors.

   D. Whales always existed in their current form, along with many other relatives.

© Houghton Mifflin Harcourt

Engineer It

Apply the Use of 3D Printing to Model Fossils

Fossils can be both fragile and tiny, making them very difficult to study. One solution to this problem is using 3D printing technology. People can use 3D printers to make copies of fossils out of sturdy materials such as plastic. They can even make copies that are smaller or larger than the original fossil. Another advantage of 3D printing is that many copies of the fossil can be made.

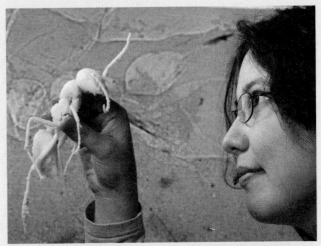

A 3D printer allows this scientist to create a large model of a tiny 100 million-year-old fossilized ant.

6. Propose at least two ways that 3D printing could help students who are interested in studying fossils but cannot access actual fossils.

Evidence of Evolutionary Relationships

Evolutionary relationships are inferred based on evidence from the fossil record. They are also inferred from similarities in the bodies of living organisms, similarities between living and fossilized organisms, and similarities among the embryos of different types of organisms. Recently, evolutionary relationships have also been studied at the genetic and molecular level. Scientists infer that the more similar species are at any level, the more closely related they are to each other.

Similarities in Anatomy

The **anatomy** of an organism is its body structure and its structural traits. Related organisms have a similar anatomy. For example, the body structures of insects are more like those of other insects than those of birds. Consider a structural trait such as feathers. It was once accepted that only birds had feathers. Soft, fluffy feathers provide insulation. Longer, sleeker feathers enable flight. But recent fossil discoveries reveal short structures in certain dinosaur fossils that look similar to certain modern bird feathers. Scientists identified these structures as feathers. These feathers provide evidence that dinosaurs and birds are more closely related to each other than was once thought.

© Houghton Mifflin Harcourt • Image Credits: ©Pascal Goetgheluck/Science Source

7. The front limbs of the bat, dolphin, horse, and cat look different from each other and are used in different ways. But the skeletal structure of the limbs is similar. Use the colors of the leg bones of the bat, dolphin, and horse to color the similar bones of the cat.

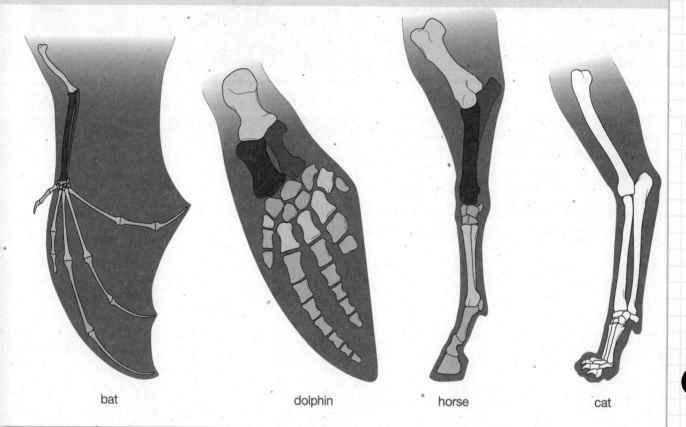

bat   dolphin   horse   cat

8. These limb bones have similar / different overall patterns of bones which can indicate a close / distant evolutionary relationship. However, the limb bones are different sizes and shapes. For example, the "finger" bones, shown in light blue and pink, are different in each animal. The form / color of the bones can help you identify the function / age of the limb.

Many four-legged organisms have similar leg structures that carry out similar functions. Similarities in anatomy can indicate evolutionary relationships. But they are not always the result of a close relationship. Some body structures evolved at different times. Some structures with similar functions also evolved in very different species. Think about the fins of whales and fish. The fins help both animals move in water. But they developed along very different evolutionary paths. So too did the wings in birds, bats, and insects. The presence and function of wings does not indicate a close evolutionary relationship between these groups of organisms because the anatomy of their wings differs so much.

 EVIDENCE NOTEBOOK

9. What anatomical structures do the *Confuciusornis* fossil and the *Corvus* (crow) share? Record your evidence.

© Houghton Mifflin Harcourt

Similarities in Embryo Development

The study of the development of unborn or unhatched organisms is called **embryology.** Embryos undergo many changes as they grow and develop. Scientists compare the embryo development of different species to look for similar patterns and structures. Based on research and observation, scientists infer that such similarities come from an ancestor that the species have in common. For example, at some time during development, all animals with backbones have a tail. This observation suggests that all animals with a backbone have a common ancestor.

Gill slits are another example of a structure that is present in the early embryos of several animal species. For example, chicken embryos and human embryos both have a stage in which they have "slits" in their necks that are similar to the gill slits of fish. The tissues that make up these gill slits develop further to become parts of the jaw, ears, and neck. Based on this and other evidence, scientists infer that chickens and humans share a common ancestor with fish. Studies of embryo development are not limited to living species. Some fossilized embryos have been found. Scientists use observations from these embryos as evidence to explain the universal process of embryo development.

Early Stages of Embryo Development

A wide range of species go through the same stages of early embryo development. These similarities indicate that these species share a common ancestor.

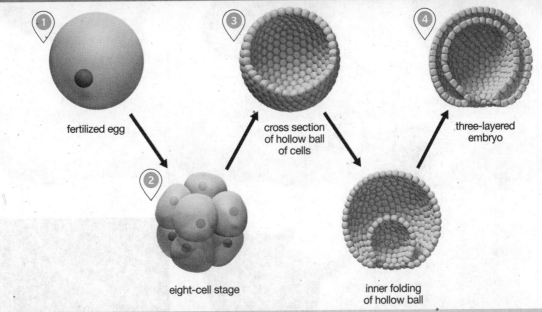

fertilized egg

cross section of hollow ball of cells

three-layered embryo

eight-cell stage

inner folding of hollow ball

① A fertilized egg contains the correct amount of genetic material needed to develop further.

② The fertilized egg soon divides into two cells. When the two cells each divide, four cells result, then eight cells. This pattern of cell division continues.

③ Eventually, a hollow ball of cells forms. At this time, certain genes are activated and others are shut down in cells, depending on where they are in the hollow ball.

④ The hollow ball eventually develops "cell layers" that go on to form internal organs and other structures.

10. Why might so many different organisms develop different traits at later stages but continue to have similar stages of early embryo development? Explain your reasoning.

© Houghton Mifflin Harcourt

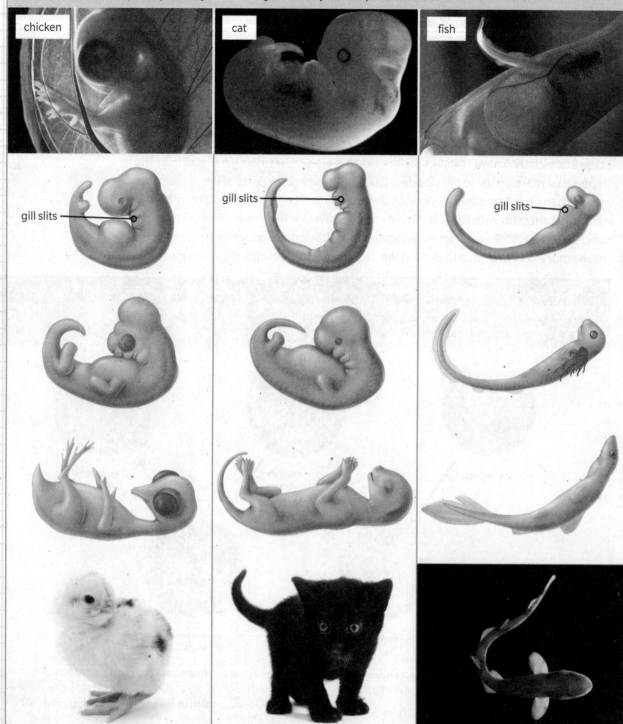

Embryo Development of Three Species

Different types of animals all go through similar stages of embryo development.

chicken

cat

fish

gill slits

gill slits

gill slits

11. Compare the structures of the cat and chicken embryos shown in the photos above. Which characteristics do the species share as embryos that they do not share when they are fully developed? Select all that apply.

   A. Both animals have gill slits as embryos.

   B. Both animals have feathers as embryos.

   C. Both animals have similar upper limb buds as embryos.

   D. Both animals have a long tail as early-stage embryos.

© Houghton Mifflin Harcourt • Image Credits: ©J. M. Labat/Visual&Written SL/Alamy; ©Manfred Kage/Science Source; ©Paulo Oliveira/Alamy; ©Anatolii/Fotolia; ©Maxim Pimenov/Fotolia; ©D.P. Wilson/FLPA/Science Source

12. What types of similarities would you expect to find in the embryo development of extinct and modern birds? Record your evidence.

Do the Math
Interpret the Geometry of Body Plans

The symmetry of an organism's body is inherited. So similarities and differences in body plans can be used to infer relatedness. Different groups of animals have characteristic body plans. For example, most animals' bodies have *bilateral symmetry*. For these animals, you could draw an imaginary line down the center of their bodies and both sides would be more or less identical to each other. Other animals have *radial symmetry*. These animals have many lines of symmetry. Sponges are an example of an organism with an *asymmetrical* body plan, which means their bodies have no symmetry.

Body Symmetry of Animals

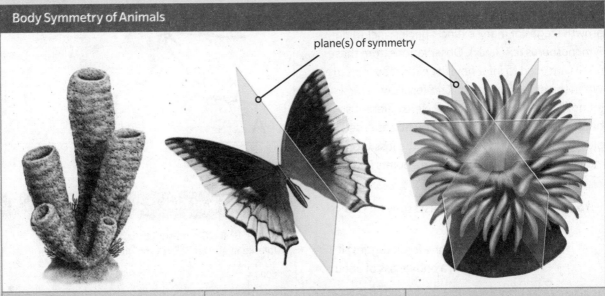

plane(s) of symmetry

| A sponge has no body symmetry. | A butterfly has bilateral symmetry. | A sea anemone has radial symmetry. |

13. The body plan of the sea slug shown in the photo has no / bilateral / radial symmetry.

14. Organisms that have similar body symmetry are considered to be more closely related to each other than to organisms with different body symmetry. Which organism in the diagram do you think this sea slug is more closely related to? Explain your answer.

_____

_____

_____

_____

© Houghton Mifflin Harcourt • Image Credits: ©Ivan Kuzmin/Alamy

Inferring Evolutionary Relationships among Organisms

Data from fossils help scientists to make inferences about extinct organisms. For example, data from fossils can be used to infer the sizes of living things, their life spans, what they ate, and how they moved. As new fossils are found, new observations are used to support, modify, or correct earlier ideas. Understanding how living things have changed over time is an ongoing process. New information adds to what scientists understand about evolutionary processes.

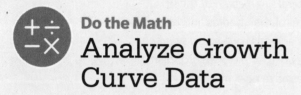

Do the Math
Analyze Growth Curve Data

Scientists have found fossils of the various growth stages of many extinct species, including *Tyrannosaurus rex* (*T. rex*). Observations from these fossils are used to infer how the extinct species grew. When the different ages of *T. rex* fossils were first found, it was thought that they were different species because they looked so different. The data used to plot the graph was collected from the fossils of seven individual *T. rex*. These are the data points in the graph.

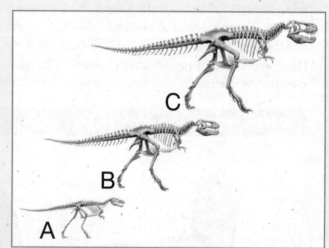

15. Imagine you are a scientist studying two different *T. rex* fossils.

    • Observations from one fossil suggest it is from a *T. rex* with a body mass of about 2,000 kg.

    • The other fossil is from a *T. rex* with a body mass of about 3,500 kg.

    Based on the growth curve data, what is the age difference between these two fossilized dinosaurs? Why can you assume the larger *T. rex* is more mature, not just bigger? Defend your answer using evidence from the graph.

Growth Curve of *T. rex*

Points A, B, and C represent the sizes of the juvenile, adolescent, and adult *T. rex* shown in the illustration.

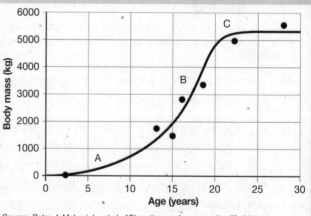

Source: Peter J. Makovicky et al., "Gigantism and comparative life-history parameters of tyrannosaurid dinosaurs," *Nature* 430, 772–775, (12 August 2004)

© Houghton Mifflin Harcourt

Hands-On Lab
Make Inferences from Evidence

You will make inferences based on visual observations. Then you will modify these inferences based on new information and data.

Scientists usually do not have all of the pieces of evidence for the topic they are studying. Instead, they work to understand the natural world by making connections, inferences, and predictions using the information they have.

> **MATERIALS**
> • picture, cut into strips

Procedure

STEP 1 Study the three strips of paper provided by your teacher. Write down all observations and inferences that you can make about this picture.

STEP 2 Make a prediction about what is shown in the picture. Use your observations to support your prediction.

STEP 3 Record observations, inferences, and a prediction as you receive each remaining strip of "new information" from your teacher.

Analysis

STEP 4 Explain how you modified your prediction about what the picture shows as you gathered more information about the picture.

STEP 5 How is this process similar to how scientists make inferences from fossil evidence? How is it different?

© Houghton Mifflin Harcourt

Lesson 3 Evidence of Common Ancestry **57**

Relationships among Fossil Organisms and Living Organisms

Body structures and other features of fossilized organisms may be similar to features present in modern organisms. In general, the more recently the fossilized organism lived, the more similar its body structures are to modern, living organisms.

Similarities and differences in anatomy are used to make inferences about evolutionary relationships among living and extinct organisms. Scientists revise and refine their understanding of evolutionary relationships as new evidence is found.

Case Study: Evolution of Elephants

Modern elephants belong to a group of mammals that includes extinct animals such as the mammoth and the mastodon. Until recently, there were only two genuses of living elephants recognized: the African elephant and the Asian elephant. Scientists closely compared the anatomy and DNA of these elephants. This evidence suggests that there are actually two different species of African elephant: the savannah elephant and the forest elephant.

Scientists have used both anatomical data and DNA analyses to make inferences about how modern elephants are related to extinct relatives. For example, scientists use tooth shape to study relatedness among elephants and their ancestors. Modern elephants have flat, ridged teeth to grind up the tough plants they eat. Like elephants, mammoths and mastodons were herbivores. They had teeth that helped them chew their food well.

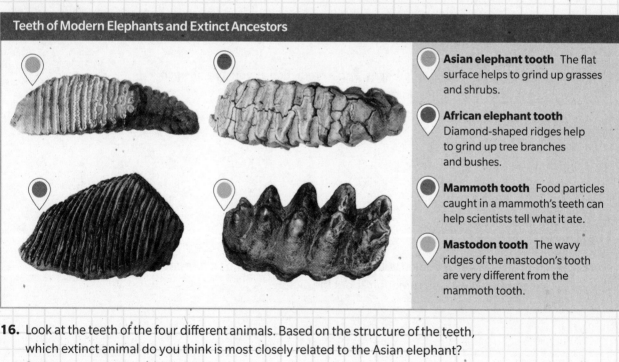

Teeth of Modern Elephants and Extinct Ancestors

Asian elephant tooth The flat surface helps to grind up grasses and shrubs.

African elephant tooth Diamond-shaped ridges help to grind up tree branches and bushes.

Mammoth tooth Food particles caught in a mammoth's teeth can help scientists tell what it ate.

Mastodon tooth The wavy ridges of the mastodon's tooth are very different from the mammoth tooth.

16. Look at the teeth of the four different animals. Based on the structure of the teeth, which extinct animal do you think is most closely related to the Asian elephant? Support your answer with evidence.

© Houghton Mifflin Harcourt • Image Credits: (t) ©Dave King/Dorling Kindersley/Getty Images; (bl) ©Colin Keates/Dorling Kindersley/Natural History Museum, London/Science; (br) ©Millard H. Sharp/Science Sourc

Elephant Lineage

The relationships in this diagram were determined by examining the anatomy of modern animals and extinct animal fossils, as well as embryological and genetic data.

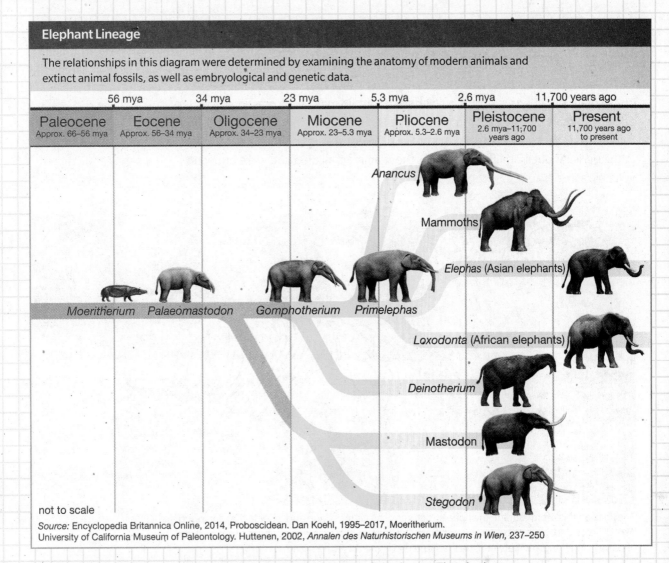

	56 mya	34 mya	23 mya	5.3 mya	2.6 mya	11,700 years ago
Paleocene Approx. 66–56 mya	**Eocene** Approx. 56–34 mya	**Oligocene** Approx. 34–23 mya	**Miocene** Approx. 23–5.3 mya	**Pliocene** Approx. 5.3–2.6 mya	**Pleistocene** 2.6 mya–11;700 years ago	**Present** 11,700 years ago to present

Anancus

Mammoths

Elephas (Asian elephants)

Moeritherium   Palaeomastodon   Gomphotherium   Primelephas

Loxodonta (African elephants)

Deinotherium

Mastodon

Stegodon

not to scale

Source: Encyclopedia Britannica Online, 2014, Proboscidean. Dan Koehl, 1995–2017, Moeritherium. University of California Museum of Paleontology. Huttenen, 2002, *Annalen des Naturhistorischen Museums in Wien,* 237–250

17. Scientists work to understand the evolutionary history of elephants. They look at embryological / anatomical data, such as tooth structure. They infer that the Asian / African elephant is most closely related to the mammoth because both animals have very similar / different tooth structures as well as other similarities.

18. Based on the diagram, which animal—extinct or alive—would you expect to have the most anatomical similarities to the mastodon? How long ago did this animal live? Explain your answer.

EVIDENCE NOTEBOOK

19. What evidence from the extinct bird fossil supports an evolutionary relationship with living bird species? Record your evidence:

© Houghton Mifflin Harcourt

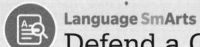
Defend a Claim with Evidence

The Ashfall Fossil Beds in northeast Nebraska contain many well-preserved fossils of ancient animals. The most common fossilized animal found there is the barrel-bodied rhinoceros (*Teleoceras major*). Fossils of five different species of horses are also found at the beds. About 12 million years ago, these animals all died and were buried in volcanic ash.

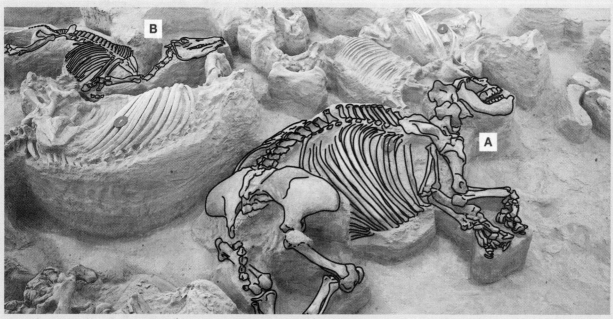

The lines on this photo outline the bone structures of an extinct rhino and a horse that are found in the Ashfall Fossil Beds. It is possible to see some of the anatomical similarities between the fossilized rhino and the living rhino and between the fossilized horse and the living horse.

Black rhinoceros (*Diceros bicornis*)

Przewalski's horse (*Equus ferus*)

20. Make a claim about which fossil, A or B, is the rhino and which fossil is the horse. Use anatomical evidence from the photos to defend your claim.

_____

_____

_____

_____

© Houghton Mifflin Harcourt • Image Credits: (t) ©Jim West/Alamy; (bl) ©Milton Griffith/ Science Source: (br) ©Vera Kuttelvaserova/Fotolia

Continue Your Exploration

Name: _____   Date: _____

Check out the path below or go online to choose one of the other paths shown.

Careers in Science	• Hands-On Labs ✋ • Classification of Living Things • Propose Your Own Path	*Go online to choose one of these other paths.*

Museum Exhibit Designer

Museum exhibit designers and educators help communicate scientific ideas to the general public through fun exhibits. Exhibit designers use creativity and innovation to share complex ideas in understandable, engaging, and interactive ways. They need a deep understanding of scientific ideas. They also need an understanding of how people learn about science and interact with museum exhibits. A successful exhibit connects with the people who go to the museum. Designers, educators, and others often collaborate to come up with new and exciting ways to share scientific ideas with learners of all ages. Today's science museums often have many opportunities for visitors to actively participate in science.

Interacting with a "living dinosaur" allows students to have fun while learning about the past.

© Houghton Mifflin Harcourt • Image Credits: ©Tommasso Boddi/Wirelmage/Getty Images

Continue Your Exploration

1. Think of a topic that you would enjoy learning about through a museum exhibit. Describe the topic and why you chose it.

2. Imagine you are an exhibit designer. Using words and drawings, describe how you would set up an exhibit about the topic you chose in order to share it with visitors.

3. What are some limitations you may need to consider while designing your exhibit?

4. **Collaborate** Work with classmates to design an exhibit about a topic from this lesson.

   - Identify the likely visitors to your exhibit (for example, third- to fifth-graders).
   - Propose one or two key messages that you want to communicate in the exhibit.
   - Describe or produce at least one interactive experience for your exhibit.
   - Share your exhibit design with others.

© Houghton Mifflin Harcourt

Can You Explain It?

Name: _____ **Date:** _____

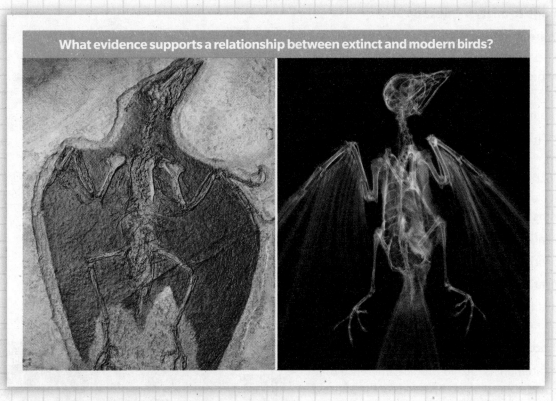

What evidence supports a relationship between extinct and modern birds?

EVIDENCE NOTEBOOK
Refer to the notes in your Evidence Notebook to help you construct an explanation of how evidence indicates that extinct and modern birds are related.

1. State your claim. Make sure your claim fully explains how the extinct and modern organisms might be related.

2. Summarize the evidence you have gathered to support your claim and explain your reasoning.

© Houghton Mifflin Harcourt • Image Credits: (l) ©Millard H. Sharp/Science Source; (r) ©D. Roberts/Science Source

Checkpoints

Answer the following questions to check your understanding of the lesson.

Use the image to answer Question 3.

3. Gill slits are structural features in cat embryos that are / are not found in a fully developed cat. The presence of gill slits is evidence that cats share a common ancestor with chickens and other organisms that have gill slits as adults/ during embryo development.

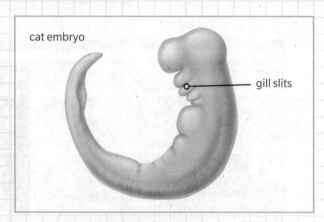

cat embryo

gill slits

4. Which of the following observations provide evidence of evolutionary relatedness among organisms? Select all that apply.

   A. similarities in body structures

   B. similarities in molecular structures

   C. similarities in embryological development

   D. similarities in the foods that organisms eat

Use the photos to answer Question 5.

5. Which statement is the most logical inference that can be made based on observations of the photos?

   A. The two organisms shown are likely related because they have similarities in leaf structure.

   B. The two organisms shown are likely related because the fossilized plant was green like the living plant.

   C. The two organisms shown are NOT likely related because one is a fossil and the other is living.

   D. The two organisms shown are NOT likely related because there is no evidence that they grow and develop in similar ways.

fossil fern

live fern

© Houghton Mifflin Harcourt • Image Credits: (c) ©Dirk Wiersma/Science Source; (b) ©djunger/Fotolia

6. Which description best explains what scientists do if new evidence is found about evolutionary relationships that is different from evidence already gathered?

   A. Scientists discard earlier ideas about the evolutionary relationships.

   B. Scientists revise their understanding about evolutionary relationships.

   C. Scientists rarely change their ideas even if new evidence is found.

   D. Scientists change evidence to fit existing ideas of evolutionary relationships.

Interactive Review

Complete this section to review the main concepts of the lesson.

Offspring look similar to their parents because heritable traits are passed down from parent to offspring. Over time, genetic changes in populations build up.

A. How can anatomy be used to study relationships among different types of organisms?

Scientists use fossil, anatomical, embryological, and genetic evidence to make inferences about evolutionary relationships.

B. Explain how inferences about evolutionary relationships can change as new evidence is discovered.

© Houghton Mifflin Harcourt • Image Credits: (t) ©john michael evan potter/Shutterstock; (b) ©Colin Keates/Dorling Kindersley/Natural History Museum, London/Science Source

Choose one of the activities to explore how this unit connects to other topics.

☐ Social Science Connection

Uncovering the Past Archaeologists study material remains of past human civilizations to learn about human history. For example, Machu Picchu, shown here, was built around 1450 in Peru. It is made up of over 150 buildings believed to have been used by Inca leaders.

Research methods that archaeologists use to find material remains, such as remote sensing, field surveys, and excavation. Prepare a presentation that includes at least three images of artifacts found at an archaeological site. Describe how they were found and what was learned from them.

☐ Art Connection

Paleoart Art that uses scientific evidence to depict prehistoric life is called *paleoart*. Some paleoart shows fossil remains, such as a complete skeleton, and other pieces show living creatures in their environment. Paleoart influences how people think about species that have been long extinct.

Research a paleoartist. Explore how the artist creates his/her work, including the kinds of scientific evidence used. Present a poster with your findings that includes three different images of the artist's work and descriptions explaining each piece.

☐ Physical Science Connection

Rock Dating Radioactive isotopes are unstable particles that break down, or *decay*, into more stable particles at a precise rate. Different radioactive isotopes decay at different rates. Scientists compare the amount of a radioactive isotope to the amount of stable particles in a rock sample to find its age.

Research a radioactive isotope that scientists use to estimate the ages of rocks. Identify the *half-life* of this isotope and the stable particles that are formed. Present a graph that shows the decay rate of the isotope over time. Use the graph to help explain what a half-life is and how scientists use the decay rate to estimate the age of the rock sample in which the isotope is found.

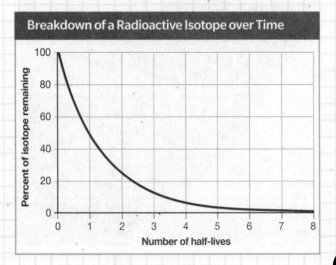

Breakdown of a Radioactive Isotope over Time

Percent of isotope remaining vs. *Number of half-lives*

© Houghton Mifflin Harcourt • Image Credits: (t) ©Rob Kroenert/Getty Images; (c) ©Mark Stevenson/Stocktrek Images/Getty Images

Name: _____   Date: _____

Complete this review to check your understanding of the unit.

Use the photo of the flowering plant fossil to answer Questions 1 and 2.

1. This fossil is about 50 million years old. What might this fossil provide evidence for? Select all that apply.

  A. the existence of flowering plants 50 million years ago

  B. the extinction of flowering plants 50 million years ago

  C. similarities in structure between ancient and modern flowering plants

  D. a common ancestor of certain types of modern flowering plants

2. Most fossil evidence of flowering plants is limited to grains of pollen. Why might it be rare for a complete plant fossil, such as this one, to form? Select all that apply.

  A. There were not many plants 50 million years ago.

  B. Wind or water can carry soft plant parts away before they fossilize.

  C. Dry environments cause plants to decay too slowly to fossilize.

  D. Flower parts are delicate and rarely experience the conditions needed to fossilize.

Use the illustration of the dolphin embryo to answer Questions 3 and 4.

3. The red circle on the dolphin embryo identifies the beginning of a hind leg structure. This embryo structure is / is·not present in the fully formed dolphin anatomy. This structure is an example of a similarity between dolphins and other mammals that is evident / not evident in the fully formed organisms.

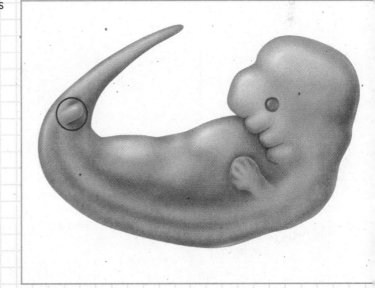

4. Which statement does this dolphin embryo structure provide evidence for?

  A. Dolphins are more closely related to other mammals with hind legs than to fish.

  B. Dolphins are more closely related to fish than to other mammals with hind legs.

  C. Dolphins do not share an evolutionary relationship with other mammals.

  D. Dolphins do not share an evolutionary relationship with fish.

© Houghton Mifflin Harcourt • Image Credits: (t) ©Xinhua/Alamy

5. Complete the table by providing at least one example of how these methods of studying the history of life on Earth relate to each big concept.

Method of Study	Pattern Used to Identify Relationships	Methods of Analyzing Data	Evidence of Common Ancestry
Finding Relative Ages of Rock Layers	Deeper rock layers are older; layers closer to the surface are more recent.		
Finding Absolute Ages of Rock Layers			
Comparing Embryo Development			
Comparing Anatomical Structures			

© Houghton Mifflin Harcourt

Name: _____   **Date:** _____

Use the graph to answer Questions 6–8.

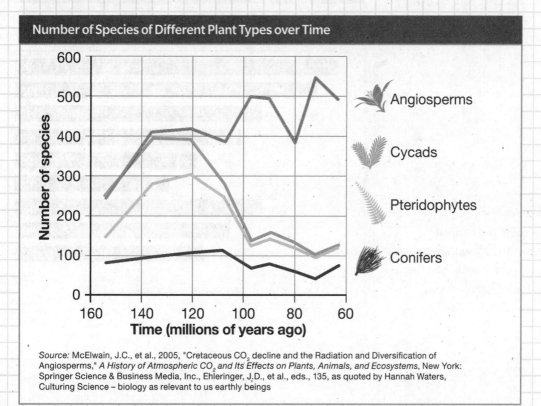

Number of Species of Different Plant Types over Time

Angiosperms

Cycads

Pteridophytes

Conifers

Source: McElwain, J.C., et al., 2005, "Cretaceous CO_2 decline and the Radiation and Diversification of Angiosperms," *A History of Atmospheric CO_2 and Its Effects on Plants, Animals, and Ecosystems*, New York: Springer Science & Business Media, Inc., Ehleringer, J.D., et al., eds., 135, as quoted by Hannah Waters, Culturing Science – biology as relevant to us earthly beings

6. Scientists use fossil data to estimate the number of species for each plant type over time. Explain how they estimate the ages of plant fossils found in different rock layers.

7. Which group of plants has had the most extinctions during the time frame shown in the graph? When did most of these extinctions occur? Explain your answer.

8. Construct an explanation for the pattern in the number of flowering plant species during the time period when many other plant species were going extinct.

© Houghton Mifflin Harcourt

Use the chart to answer Questions 9–12.

9. Which group of organisms represented in this graphic appears earliest in the fossil record? Which group appears most recently?

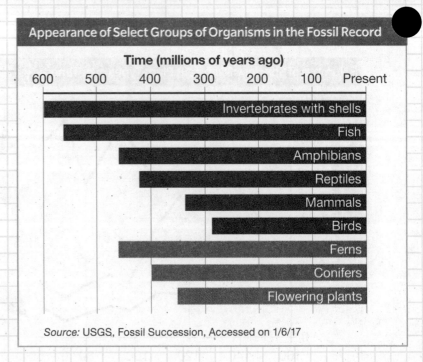

Appearance of Select Groups of Organisms in the Fossil Record

Time (millions of years ago)

600   500   400   300   200   100   Present

Invertebrates with shells
Fish
Amphibians
Reptiles
Mammals
Birds
Ferns
Conifers
Flowering plants

Source: USGS, Fossil Succession, Accessed on 1/6/17

10. Would you expect the earliest mammal fossils to be found in deeper or shallower layers of rock than the earliest fern fossils? Explain your reasoning.

11. Describe how this graphic provides evidence for the general pattern of increasing diversity of life over time.

12. Only multicellular organisms are represented in this graphic. Given that most fossils older than 500 million years are single celled marine organisms, describe the changes in the level of complexity of organisms in the fossil record over time.

© Houghton Mifflin Harcourt

Name: _____   Date: _____

Which species is more closely related to the red panda?

Examine the images of the red panda and the *Parailurus*. The *Parailurus* has been extinct for about three million years. Scientists have discovered fossil remains of the *Parailurus* in Japan, North America, and Europe. The *Parailurus* is the closest ancestor of the red panda, but what is the red panda's closest living relative? Some scientists have classified the red panda with the giant panda, others have classified it with the raccoon family. Use evidence to make a claim about which of these living species is likely more closely related to the red panda.

red panda

Parailurus

The steps below will help guide your research and develop your explanation.

1. **Ask Questions** How can an extinct species be an ancestor to a living species? Why would you expect organisms with similar anatomy to be more closely related? What questions do you have about the red panda that might help you determine its closest living relative?

2. **Conduct Research** Find information about the anatomy of the red panda, the giant panda, and the raccoon, including their sizes.

© Houghton Mifflin Harcourt • Image Credits: ©DLILLC/Cardinal/Corbis

3. **Develop Diagrams** Create diagrams that illustrate the anatomical structures and relative sizes of the red panda, the giant panda, and the raccoon.

4. **Analyze Diagrams** Use the diagrams to identify anatomical similarities and differences among the three living species.

5. **Construct an Explanation** Write an explanation as to whether the giant panda or the raccoon is likely the closest living relative to the red panda. Use evidence from your analysis of anatomical structures and a description of the relationship between genetic makeup and anatomy to support your reasoning.

✓ **Self-Check**

	I explained how an extinct species can be an ancestor to a living species.
	I conducted research on the red panda, giant panda, and raccoon.
	I developed diagrams to compare the anatomies of the red panda, the giant panda, and the raccoon.
	I analyzed my diagrams to identify anatomical similarities and differences.
	I constructed an explanation based on an analysis of anatomical structures.

© Houghton Mifflin Harcourt

Evolution

The Galápagos prickly pear cactus is common on the Galápagos islands, but they do not live anywhere else on Earth. Small finches build their nests between the prickly cactus pads.

Have you ever wondered about the wide variety of organisms on Earth? Even within a single species, there is much variation. In fact, on the Galápagos Islands, there are six different species of prickly pear cactus! Each of these species has the characteristic prickly "pads," but there are differences in the overall size, pad shape, pad color, and spines. How did all of this variation come to exist? In this unit, you will explore the effects of genetic mutation on organisms. You will also investigate how natural selection can lead to changes in populations and explain how these changes can result in new species.

© Houghton Mifflin Harcourt • Image Credits: ©Layne Kennedy/Corbis Documentary/ Getty Images

Why It Matters

Here are some questions to consider as you work through the unit. Can you answer any of the questions now? Revisit these questions at the end of the unit to apply what you discover.

Questions	Notes
What causes the different traits we observe in living things?	
How can populations adapt to changes in the environment over time?	
Can some types of changes in populations be predicted?	
How can humans influence the resistance of insects to pesticides and bacteria to antibiotics?	
How can new species arise and other species die out?	

© Houghton Mifflin Harcourt

Unit Starter: Applying the Concept of Probability

The likelihood, or *probability*, of being seen is greater in the dark if you wear light clothing instead of dark clothing. The same idea applies in nature with predator-prey relationships. The probability of being seen by predators can be affected by how well an animal blends in with its environment. Look at the images of rock pocket mice, a mouse species that lives in the Sonoran Desert.

Some rock pocket mice have dark-colored fur and live amongst light-colored rocks.

Some rock pocket mice have dark-colored fur and live amongst dark volcanic rocks.

Some rock pocket mice have light-colored fur and live amongst dark volcanic rocks.

Some rock pocket mice have light-colored fur and live amongst light-colored rocks.

1. A mouse with dark / light fur would have a greater probability of being seen and eaten by a predator among light-colored rocks. Therefore, in the light-colored environment, mice with dark fur have an increased / decreased probability of survival compared to mice with light fur.

2. Based on the probabilities of survival for mice with dark and light fur in the different environments, there would likely be more mice with dark / light fur in the light-colored environment, and more mice with dark / light fur in the dark-colored environment.

Go online to download the Unit Project Worksheet to help you plan your project

Unit Project

Real-World Example of Natural Selection

Choose a real-world example of natural selection to research. Explain why some individuals had a greater probability of surviving and reproducing in the environment. Use data from your research to illustrate how certain traits have increased in the population over time while other traits decreased, and make predictions about how other traits might change in the future.

© Houghton Mifflin Harcourt

Genetic Change and Traits

The black color of this jaguar is the result of a gene that controls the dark pigment in the jaguar's fur.

By the end of this lesson . . .

you will be able to explain how changes to genes affect traits in an organism.

© Houghton Mifflin Harcourt • Image Credits: ©Sterbennett/iStock/Getty Images Plus/ Getty Images

Go online to view the digital version of the Hands-On Lab for this lesson and to download additional lab resources.

CAN YOU EXPLAIN IT?

How can a change to just one gene cause a lobster to be blue?

Only 1 in about 2 million lobsters is blue. The blue color is the result of a rare genetic mutation.

1. Identify at least three other body features of these lobsters. How do you think a change to the lobster's genes could have an affect on any of these features?

© Houghton Mifflin Harcourt • Image Credits: (l) ©Gary Lewis/Photolibrary/Getty Images; (r) ©Andrew J. Martinez/Science Source

 EVIDENCE NOTEBOOK As you explore the lesson, gather evidence to help explain how a change to a gene can result in a blue lobster.

Describing the Relationship Between Genes and Traits

Observe the students in your classroom. They share many traits, but they do not look exactly the same. Some traits can be inherited, such as eye color and face shape. Inherited traits are passed on from parents to offspring by genetic material. Other traits, such as language and musical taste, are determined by the environment. However, most traits are influenced by both genetic and environmental factors. Each person has a unique combination of many traits.

The differences in eye colors, face shapes, and smiles of these students is due to differences in traits.

DNA Is the Genetic Material in Cells

The genetic material in organisms is **DNA.** It is a double-stranded molecule organized into structures called *chromosomes*. In organisms that reproduce sexually, cells have pairs of chromosomes. The offspring receives one chromosome from each of the two parents. A DNA molecule contains the information that determines the traits that an organism inherits. DNA also contains the instructions for an organism's growth and development.

2. **Discuss** How might an inherited trait, such as height, be influenced by both genetic and environmental factors?

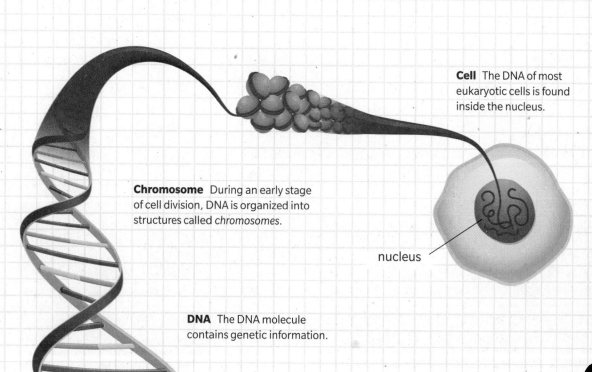

Cell The DNA of most eukaryotic cells is found inside the nucleus.

Chromosome During an early stage of cell division, DNA is organized into structures called *chromosomes*.

nucleus

DNA The DNA molecule contains genetic information.

© Houghton Mifflin Harcourt ©Christopher Futcher/iStock/Getty Images Plus/Getty Images

Genes Are Segments of DNA

Each side, or strand, of DNA is a chain of building blocks called *nucleotides*. These repeating chemical units join together to form a DNA molecule. One part of a nucleotide is called the *base*. There are four different nucleotides in DNA, which are identified by their bases: adenine (A), guanine (G), cytosine (C), and thymine (T). Where the two strands connect, A pairs with T and G pairs with C. These paired bases fit together like the pieces of a puzzle.

Nucleotides line up so that the DNA backbone is like the handrail of a ladder. The bases—A, T, C, and G—join to make the rungs of the ladder.

Combinations of alphabet letters make meaningful words. Likewise, combinations of DNA base pairs make "genetic words" called *genes*. A **gene** is a specific segment of DNA that provides instructions for an inherited trait. Each gene has a starting point and an ending point. DNA is read in one direction, just as you read words from left to right. Genes are responsible for the inherited traits of an organism. Organisms that reproduce sexually have two versions of the same gene for every trait—one version from each parent.

3. Complete the DNA sequence by adding complementary bases to the DNA strand. You may draw using colors or write letters to represent the nucleotide bases.

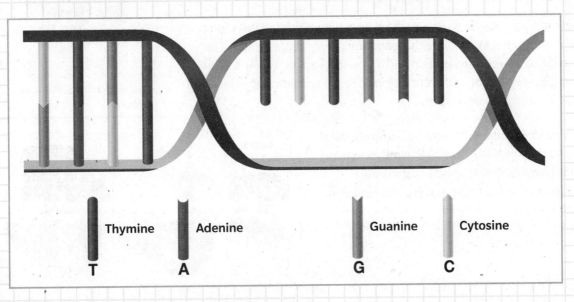

© Houghton Mifflin Harcourt

Genes Code for Proteins

A **protein** is an important molecule that is needed to build and repair body structures and to control processes in the body. Proteins are made up of smaller molecules called *amino acids*. About 20 different kinds of amino acids combine to make proteins. A specific sequence of three bases on a gene codes for a specific amino acid. These sequences are called *triplets*. The chain of amino acids produced by a gene depends on the order of the triplets. In this way, the genes of a chromosome carry the instructions for the proteins that are made by cells.

Relate DNA Code to Protein Production

4. The diagram on the left shows the triplet codes for six amino acids. Use the diagram to complete the triplets and amino acids on the right.

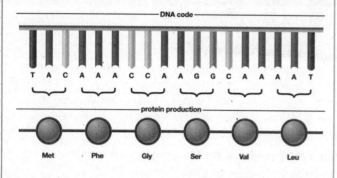

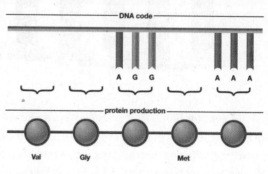

Once built, the amino acid chain twists and folds to form the protein's three-dimensional shape. A protein's shape is linked to its function. For example, collagen is a protein that folds into a long, fiber-like chain. It strengthens skin. Other proteins, called *hormones*, deliver messages to cells by fitting into specific locations on target cells like a key in a lock.

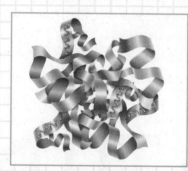

Amino acid chains fold and link together to form the 3D structure of a protein.

5. Some triplets code for the same amino acid. Sometimes, a DNA triplet is exchanged for another one that codes for the same amino acid. The function of the resulting protein will / will not be affected. If the DNA triplet codes for a different amino acid, the function of the protein will / will not be affected.

6. *Enzymes* are proteins that help speed up chemical reactions in the body. They often work by binding to target molecules. How do you think the sequence of amino acids in an enzyme relates to its ability to bind to a specific target molecule?

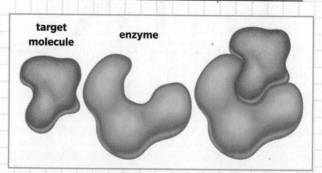

The active site of an enzyme has just the right shape to bind to the target molecule.

© Houghton Mifflin Harcourt

Hands-On Lab
Model Protein Folding

You will use paper strips to model protein folding.

Amino acid chains fold or twist when one region of the chain is attracted to, or repelled by, another region. This folding or twisting depends on the chemical structure of each amino acid, as well as how close they are together in the chain.

MATERIALS
- colored pencils, red, blue, green
- paper strips, white, 1 inch wide and 12 inches long (2)
- ruler

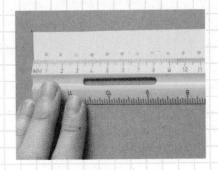

Procedure

STEP 1 Consider the amino acid sequence below. On the strip of white paper, draw colored dots indicated by the sequence using corresponding colors—red, blue, or green. Use the ruler to help you leave a 1 cm space between each dot.

Amino acid sequence 1:

His – Lys – Ser – Gly – Ala – Gly – Cys – Pro – Ser – Asp – Val – Leu – Met – Gly – Thr – Pro – Gly – Ala – Cys – Asp – Met

STEP 2 Fold your amino acid chain into a three-dimensional protein by following the guidelines below. Work from one end of the white paper strip to the other. Try to fold halfway between the relevant colored dots when folding.

- Same color next to each other—no fold
- **Red** next to green—90° fold down
- **Red** next to blue—90° fold up (dotted sides of strip come together)
- **Blue** next to green—45° airplane fold (colored dots come together with a diagonal crease)

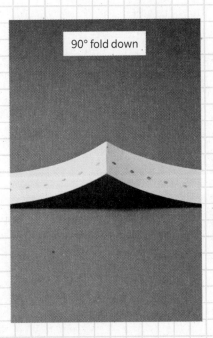

90° fold down

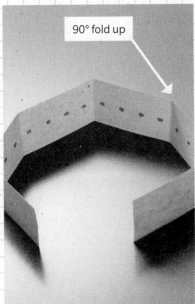

90° fold up

45° airplane fold

© Houghton Mifflin Harcourt • Image Credits: (t, bl, bc, br) ©HMH

Analysis

STEP 3 Once you have folded your protein, observe its shape. Then set it aside to compare with other proteins you will make.

STEP 4 Now consider the next amino acid sequence. Following the same procedure as you did for the first sequence, complete the three-dimensional protein.

Amino acid sequence 2:

His – Lys – Ser – Gly – Ala – Gly – Cys – Pro – Ser – Asp – His – Leu – Met – Gly – Thr – Pro – Gly – Ala – Cys – Asp – Met

STEP 5 Compare the two amino acid sequences. What is the difference between the two sequences?

STEP 6 How did the change in the amino acid sequence affect protein structure?

STEP 7 Do you think the proteins formed by the different amino acid sequences can still perform the same function?

📋 **EVIDENCE NOTEBOOK**

7. How might the change in the folding pattern of the paper strip proteins relate to the genetic change that causes a lobster to be blue? Record your evidence.

© Houghton Mifflin Harcourt

Proteins Affect Traits

Different versions of the same gene can result in proteins with different structures and properties. Proteins do much of the chemical work inside cells, so they are largely responsible for traits. The variety in proteins results in the variety of traits we see in organisms. For example, Labrador Retrievers are dogs that show a variety of coat colors. The coat will be brown or black depending on which protein is coded for in the pigment gene. When a different protein inactivates the brown or black coat pigment gene, Labradors have yellow coats.

 Language SmArts

Illustrate the Flow of Genetic Information

Scientists have modified tomato plant genes to produce the same pigments that give blackberries their dark color and health benefits. The result—purple tomatoes!

8. **Draw** Use the terms protein, gene, trait, and amino acids to make a diagram or concept map that shows the flow of genetic information that causes purple tomatoes.

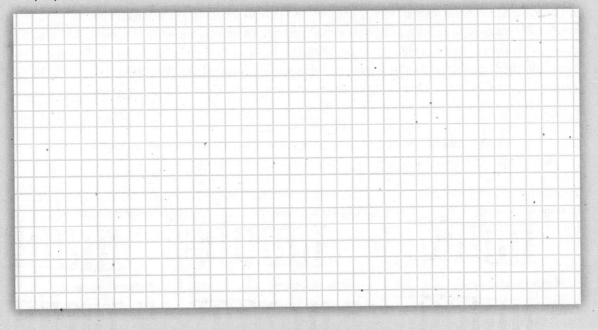

9. Using your completed diagram, write a summary of the relationship between genes, proteins, and traits.

_____

_____

_____

_____

_____

© Houghton Mifflin Harcourt ©John Innes/Handout/Getty Images

Exploring the Causes of Genetic Change

Leaf-like scales distinguish the bush viper from its smooth-skinned snake relatives. Keratin proteins shape scales. They arrange in ridges instead of smooth rows. What caused this new trait to appear in bush vipers? The ridged scale pattern in bush vipers is due to genetic changes that result in changes to proteins.

10. Which of the following outcomes could also result from a change in one of the bush viper's genes? Select all that apply.

   A. no effect on traits

   B. a genetic disease

   C. a new skin color

The African bush viper lives in tropical forests. Its scales help it camouflage within the bright green foliage.

Mutations

A change in the base-pair sequence of a gene is called a **mutation.** Most mutations occur when a cell copies its DNA for cell division. As the DNA is copied, base pairs may be added, removed, or substituted. These chance mutations may be beneficial, neutral, or harmful to organisms. For example, a mutation that results in longer fangs may be beneficial if it helps the bush viper grab prey. Mutations can also occur when DNA is exposed to *mutagens*, substances that cause genetic mutations. Examples of mutagens include UV radiation and the chemicals in cigarette smoke.

11. Study the DNA base sequences. On the line provided, record whether the mutation is the result of a base that was added, removed, or substituted.

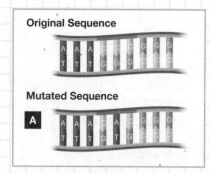

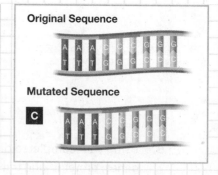

A. _____   **B.** _____   **C.** _____

12. Consider that DNA is read as triplets as proteins are built. Which mutation types might have the biggest effect on protein structure? Explain your answer.

© Houghton Mifflin Harcourt: ©Mark Kostich/iStock/Getty Images Plus/Getty Images

13. Look again at the enzyme diagram and its target molecule. How might a mutation affect the interaction between the enzyme and its target and the function of the enzyme in the organism?

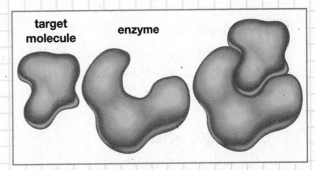

target molecule   enzyme

The target molecule and the enzyme are both proteins. Their 3D shapes are determined by the order of their amino acids.

Body Cells and Reproductive Cells

Mutations can occur in the DNA of body cells. They can also occur in the DNA of reproductive cells—eggs and sperm. When cells divide, mutations are passed on with the genetic material into the new cell. Only mutations that occur in the DNA of reproductive cells can be passed on from parent to offspring.

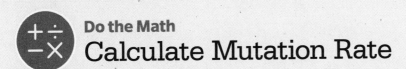

Do the Math
Calculate Mutation Rate

Organisms must copy their DNA to reproduce. Mutations can occur any time DNA is copied. Many of these mutations are corrected by cells. However, sometimes a mutation is not corrected and becomes part of the genetic code of a species.

DNA Mutations Over Time		
Mutations (shown in black) tend to add up at a fairly constant rate in the DNA of a particular species.	**Original DNA sequence**	G A A C G T A T T C A G G T C T
	5 million years later	G A A C G T A T T C A G G T C T
	10 million years later	G T A C G T A T T C A G G T C T
	15 million years later	G T A A G T A T T C A C G T C T
	20 million years later	G T A A G T A T T C A C G T C T
	25 million years later	G T A A G A A T T C A C G T C T

14. How many mutations accumulated in this DNA sequence over 25 million years?

15. Based on these data, estimate the mutation rate for this DNA sequence over 100 million years.

© Houghton Mifflin Harcourt

16. What are the connections between mutation, protein structure and function, and the lobster's blue color? Record your evidence.

Sexual Reproduction

Sexual reproduction, like mutation, is a source of genetic change. One or more genes can get reshuffled among chromosomes when the egg and sperm form. Since the shuffling of genes is random, each egg or sperm will carry a different set of chromosomes. This explains differences among offspring that come from the same parents.

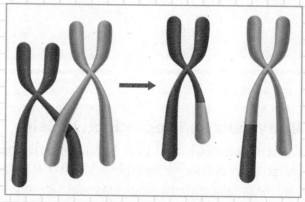

Chromosomes from the mother (purple) and father (green) can "cross over" when the egg and sperm combine, allowing large segments of DNA to swap locations.

17. When DNA segments switch places during egg or sperm formation, it can affect *only one / several* gene(s).

Engineer It
Identify Design Solution Constraints

Earth's atmosphere includes a thin layer of *ozone*, a compound that absorbs UV rays coming from the sun. UV light can cause mutations in DNA. It causes neighboring thymine bases on the same strand to break their bonds with adenine and bond with each other instead. Human-generated pollutants break down ozone in the atmosphere, putting people at higher risk of sunburn and skin cancer.

Earth's ozone layer can be seen from space. It lies within the thin blue band of the outer atmosphere .

18. According to the paragraph, pollution causes the ozone layer to *thin / expand*. As a result, living organisms have a *higher / lower* risk of UV damage. This represents an engineering problem for which *a solution / an experiment* can be designed to help reduce ozone depletion.

19. Which of the following are constraints that should be considered in designing solutions to this problem? Select all that apply.

  A. The solution must result in a cure for skin cancer.

  B. The solution must not cause harm to living organisms.

  C. The solution must be cost-effective.

  D. The solution must not cause an imbalance of other atmospheric gases.

© Houghton Mifflin Harcourt • Image Credits: ©Aleksandar Vrzalski/E+/Getty Images

Explaining the Relationship Between Genetic Change and Adaptation

The star-nosed mole is the fastest mammal forager on Earth. A ring of twenty-two finger-like projections around its snout helps the mole detect and capture prey in a fraction of a second. Long ago, genetic change causing nose segments to remain separated was passed from one mole to its offspring. The offspring were able to find prey better than other moles in the population. These offspring reproduced successfully, passing the mutation to their offspring also. Over many generations, this segmented structure became common in the population.

20. Do you think the genetic change that resulted in the segmented nose occurred in the DNA of body cells or the DNA of reproductive cells? Why?

Star-nosed moles mostly eat earthworms and aquatic insects.

Genetic Change and Adaptation

Genetic changes resulting from mutation and sexual reproduction lead to different traits in the individuals of a population. Traits that help organisms survive and reproduce in their current environment are called **adaptations.** An adaptation can be a structure, a function, or a behavior. For example, the structure of the star-nosed mole's nose allows it to locate prey more effectively than a rounded nose. Specialized nervous system function allows the moles to process information from their environment very rapidly. When star-nosed moles search for food, they constantly touch the environment with the star—between 10 and 15 places every second. This behavior helps them to rapidly detect and capture small prey. The adaptations of the star-nosed mole are the result of genetic change, inheritance of adaptive traits, and survival advantage in an environment over many generations.

EVIDENCE NOTEBOOK

21. Do you think that the mutation that causes the blue color of the lobster is inherited? Record your evidence.

© Houghton Mifflin Harcourt • Image Credits: ©Skip Moody/Science Source

Identify Adaptations

22. Read the description of each organism. In the space provided, list one structure, function, or behavior that you think is an adaptation. Then briefly explain how this adaptation benefits the organism.

	The barrel cactus lives in dry, hot deserts. It has a round stem covered with spines. The flowers bloom when temperatures drop and pollinators are plentiful.	
	The scorpion has a tough exoskeleton and poison in its curled tail. It is well armed for life in the desert. It will burrow in the sand to escape the scorching heat.	
	The ocelot hunts a variety of prey, including rodents, iguanas, and monkeys. It has a unique patterned coat, sharp eyesight, and sharp teeth. The ocelot is active mostly at night.	

Relate Traits to the Environment

The mountain goat is well adapted to its environment. It has a compact body covered in thick fur, split hooves, strong rear legs, and a narrow snout. It lives on steep, rocky slopes where temperatures can drop well below zero. Plants on these slopes grow only a few inches tall in the shallow, nutrient-poor soil.

The mountain goat's round, compact body helps it to retain water and heat.

23. Draw Suppose climate change affects the mountain goat's environment. Longer summers and increased rainfall allow insects to thrive and plants to grow tall and cover rocks. What new traits might help the mountain goat adapt to these changes in its environment? Sketch a mountain goat with a new, adaptive trait and explain how this trait could arise in the population.

© Houghton Mifflin Harcourt • Image Credits: (t) ©Randimal/Shutterstock; (tcl) ©heckepics/ iStock/Getty Images Plus/Getty Images; (bcl) ©Berndt Fischer/Photographer's Choice/ Getty Images (b) ©joshschutz/Fotolia

Continue Your Exploration

Name: _____ Date: _____

Check out the path below or go online to choose one of the other paths shown.

Mutation and Phenotype

- **Hands-On Labs** ✋
- **Mutagens**
- **Propose Your Own Path**

Go online to choose one of these other paths.

Phenotype refers to the observable traits of an organism. It is determined by the combination of genes the organism has and, sometimes, by environmental factors. Mutations can result in different gene versions for a trait, resulting in a variety of phenotypes. Flower color, skin patterns, and behaviors, such as nest building, are a few examples of phenotypes. A particular phenotype can be an advantage or disadvantage, depending on the environment where the organism lives.

Migaloo is the only recorded albino humpback whale.

1. Look at the photo of the albino whale people have named Migaloo. The white color is the result of mutations in the genes that code for the proteins responsible for skin color. Is Migaloo's white color likely to be an advantage in its current environment? Explain your answer.

© Houghton Mifflin Harcourt • Image Credits: ©REX/Jenny Dean/AP Images

Continue Your Exploration

2. The sickle cell mutation negatively affects the function of a protein called *hemoglobin*. This molecule in red blood cells delivers oxygen throughout the body. Describe the relationship between the sickle cell phenotype and hemoglobin's structure and function.

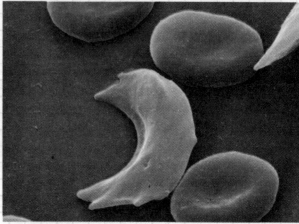

A mutation results in a "sickle" blood cell phenotype instead of a round blood cell phenotype.

3. The folded ears of a Scottish Fold cat do not interfere with the cat's ability to hear. However, the same mutation is also associated with bone and joint problems. Would you consider the mutation that causes the folded ear phenotype to be harmful, neutral, or beneficial for the Scottish Fold? Explain your answer.

A mutation that affects tissue development is responsible for the folded ear phenotype of the Scottish Fold cat.

4. Can a gene mutation that does not influence phenotype be considered an adaptation? Why or why not?

5. **Collaborate** Work with a partner to research a plant or animal that lives in your area. Describe its current traits and brainstorm five chance mutations that could occur. Discuss how each mutation might affect the organism—would it be helpful, harmful, or have no effect on the organism's ability to survive in the current environment? Then think of a change that could occur to the environment. Explain how any of these same mutations might be more helpful or harmful in the changed environment. Present your adaptation story using an animation, storyboard, or short video.

© Houghton Mifflin Harcourt • Image Credits: (t) ©Eye of Science/Science Source; (b) ©Megaloman1ac/Fotolia

Can You Explain It?

Name: _____ Date: _____

How can a change to just one gene cause a lobster to be blue?

EVIDENCE NOTEBOOK

Refer to the notes in your Evidence Notebook to help you construct an explanation for how a change to a single gene can cause a lobster to be blue.

1. State your claim. Make sure your claim fully explains how a change to one gene can cause the blue phenotype in lobsters.

2. Summarize the evidence you have gathered to support your claim and explain your reasoning.

© Houghton Mifflin Harcourt • Image Credits: (l) ©Gary Lewis/Photolibrary/Getty Images; (r) ©Andrew J. Martinez/Science Source

Checkpoints

Answer the following questions to check your understanding of the lesson.

Use the photo of the betta fish to answer Question 3.

3. A gene mutation in the betta fish results in a double-tail. In this example, the mutation results in a change to a *physical trait / behavior*. This change is desirable by fish breeders but does not provide a survival advantage for the fish, so it *is / is not* considered an adaptation.

4. Which sequence best explains the relationship between DNA and protein structure and function?

   A. DNA → gene → protein → trait

   B. DNA → amino acid triplets → protein → trait

   C. DNA base triplets → amino acid sequence → protein folding pattern → protein shape and function

   D. DNA shape → amino acid sequence → protein shape and function

Use the photo of the bee-eater to answer Questions 5 and 6.

5. Bee-eaters are birds that eat insects, especially bees and wasps. They grab flying prey from the air with their beaks. Long ago, genetic changes that resulted in *shorter / longer* beaks were advantageous for the bee-eater.

6. Which statement correctly connects the bee-eater's adaptations with its environment?

   A. The environment determines which bee-eater traits are adaptive.

   B. The bee-eater's traits influence where it chooses to live.

   C. The bee-eater's adaptive traits will not change as the environment changes.

   D. The environment has no relationship to the bee-eater's adaptive traits.

© Houghton Mifflin Harcourt • Image Credits: (t) ©halimqd/Shutterstock; (b) ©Javier Castro/Fotolia

Interactive Review

Complete this section to review the main concepts of the lesson.

Genes in DNA code for proteins that determine an organism's traits.

A. Describe how genes are related to the structure and function of proteins.

Mutations and sexual reproduction are causes of genetic change.

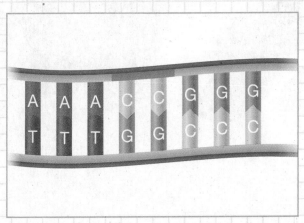

B. Explain how mutations to genes can affect traits in organisms.

Traits that help organisms survive or reproduce in their current environment are called adaptations.

C. Explain the relationship between genetic change and adaptation.

© Houghton Mifflin Harcourt • Image Credits: (t) ©Christopher Futcher/iStock/Getty Images Plus/Getty Images; (b) ©Randimal/Shutterstock

Natural Selection

A manta ray uses long fins on each side of its head to funnel tiny organisms into its mouth. This adaptation helps manta rays gather enough food to support their huge size.

By the end of this lesson . . .

you will be able to explain the link between adaptation and natural selection.

© Houghton Mifflin Harcourt • Image Credits: ©haveseen/iStock/Getty Images Plus/Getty Images

Go online to view the digital version of the Hands-On Lab for this lesson and to download additional lab resources.

CAN YOU EXPLAIN IT?

How has the smell of rotting flesh become an adaptation for the rafflesia flower?

Rafflesia flowers smell like rotting flesh, attracting flies and other insect pollinators.

1. Flowers of many plants produce scents. A flower can smell sweet, fruity, musty, or spicy. How do you think having a specific flower scent benefits a plant?

© Houghton Mifflin Harcourt • Image Credits: ©Fadil Aziz/Corbis Documentary/ Getty Images

EVIDENCE NOTEBOOK As you explore the lesson, gather evidence to help explain how the rotting flesh smell became an adaptation for the rafflesia flower.

Relating Genetic Variation to the Distribution of Traits

The three-toed sloth and the nine-banded armadillo look very different from each other, but they share a common ancestor that lived millions of years ago. Genetic change over many generations resulted in these two species. Three-toed sloths have strong arms and sharp claws, adaptations that allow them to live in trees. Armor-like plates provide protection for armadillos, which live on the forest floor. How did these adaptations arise? **Evolution** is the change in the inherited traits of a population over many generations. On a small scale, evolution leads to the adaptation of a population to its environment. On a large scale, evolution leads to the amazing diversity of life on Earth. But in order for evolution to occur, a population must have genetic variation.

three-toed sloth

nine-banded armadillo

2. **Discuss** Construct an explanation to describe how these two species may have evolved from a common ancestor. Include mutation, adaptation, and environmental factors in your explanation.

Variation in Populations

All organisms of the same species that live in the same geographical area make up a *population*. **Variation** refers to differences between organisms in a population. This variation can be differences in physical features, behaviors, or any other characteristic that is measurable. *Genetic variation* refers to different types of genes in a population for an inherited characteristic, such as flower color or tail length. For evolution to occur in a population, there must be genetic variation in some of the traits present in the population. Genetic variation can be introduced in a population through gene mutations and the movement of individuals between populations. It can also be introduced by new combinations of genes formed during the process of sexual reproduction.

© Houghton Mifflin Harcourt • Image Credits: (l) ©Roy Toft/National Geographic/Getty Images; (r) ©sdbower/Fotolia

Do the Math
Calculate Allele Frequencies

Different forms of the same gene are called *alleles*. Biologists study how populations evolve by measuring allele frequencies. An **allele frequency** is a measurement of how common a certain allele is in a population. Evolution occurs when an allele frequency changes in a population from one generation to the next.

Mongolian gerbils can be agouti (brown) or black, depending on the combination of alleles they inherit for fur color. The combination of inherited alleles is called a *genotype*. The genotype determines the organism's *phenotype*, or physical characteristics, such as fur color.

3. A population of 200 Mongolian gerbils living near Russia's Lake Baikal includes 80 brown gerbils with the *AA* genotype, 64 brown gerbils with the *Aa* genotype, and 56 black gerbils with the *aa* genotype. Use this information to complete the table.

Genotype	Number of individuals	Number of *A* alleles	Number of *a* alleles
AA			
Aa			
aa			
Total number of each allele			
Total number of alleles (A+a)			

The frequency of an allele can be found by first writing a ratio that compares the number of that allele in the population to the total number of alleles in the population. For example:

Frequency of the *A* allele = $\dfrac{\text{number of } A \text{ alleles in population}}{\text{total number of alleles in population}}$

4. Calculate the frequency of the *A* (brown) allele and the frequency of the *a* (black) allele.

5. Mongolian gerbils are prey for sharp-eyed hawks. If a wildfire blackens the landscape, the frequency of the *a* allele for black fur color will likely increase / decrease compared to the *A* allele for brown fur color.

© Houghton Mifflin Harcourt

Distribution of Traits

Genetic variation causes differences in traits. Some traits may have only one or two possible phenotypes. Other traits may have a wide range of possible phenotypes. For example, wild lupine flowers can be purple, white, blue, violet, or purple-pink. The frequency of each flower color in a lupine population can be shown in a graph. This type of graph shows the *distribution* of different phenotypes for the flower color trait.

lupines

Color Distribution of Lupine Flowers

This graph shows the distribution of flower color for a population of wild lupine. Biologists might compare this graph with one made in the past to study how flower color in the lupine population may be changing.

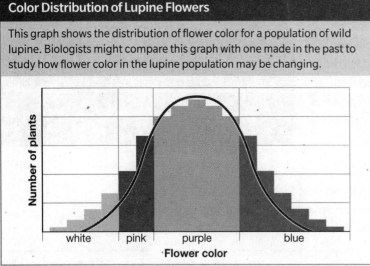

Number of plants

white   pink   purple   blue

Flower color

6. Study the distribution graph for wild lupines. Which statement could be defended using data from the graph?

   A. The population has only one allele for flower color.

   B. Conditions in the environment favor purple lupines.

   C. All flower color alleles have an equal chance of appearing in the next lupine generation.

   D. There are fewer pink and white lupines due to drought.

EVIDENCE NOTEBOOK

7. Think of odor strength as a range of phenotypes (weak to strong) in the rafflesia population. What might the distribution of traits look like on a graph? Record your evidence.

Describe Trait Distribution

Monkey flowers are found in a variety of colors ranging from white to pink to red. Animals, such as bees and hummingbirds, help these plants reproduce by transferring pollen as they travel from flower to flower. Hummingbirds prefer to visit red monkey flowers. Bumblebees prefer to visit pink flowers.

8. What do you think the distribution of color in monkey flowers would look like in a habitat that has a large population of bees and few hummingbirds?

© Houghton Mifflin Harcourt • Image Credits: (t) ©robert cicchetti/Shutterstock; (b) ©William Leaman/Alamy

Modeling Natural Selection

The distribution of traits in a population can change over time. Sometimes, a sudden change in the environment can change a distribution of traits in a random way. For example, after a wildfire there might randomly be mostly blue flowers in a lupine population. Other distribution changes are not due to chance and may be predicted using evidence. For example, a newly arrived butterfly population prefers to pollinate white lupine. It is reasonable to predict that lupine color will shift toward white in future generations.

9. The conehead katydid is an insect that can be either brown or green in color. They are eaten by a variety of predators, including birds, bats, and lizards. What are some random factors that might change the distribution of the two phenotypes? What are some nonrandom factors that might change the distribution?

conehead katydid

Natural Selection

Genetic variation determines the traits possible in a population. However, a population's current environment determines if any of those traits provide advantages or disadvantages. For example, the ability for the horned lizard to squirt toxic blood from its eyes helps the lizard avoid becoming a meal for a coyote. However, a coyote with very strong legs might be able to run fast enough to attack the lizard by surprise. **Natural selection** is a process by which a population's environment determines which traits are beneficial and which are not.

Evolution by natural selection occurs in populations, not individuals. Individuals with traits that are advantageous in an environment are better able to survive and reproduce. These traits get passed on more often to the next generation than less helpful traits. Evolution occurs as a population's genes and their frequencies change over time. While evolution can occur by several different processes, natural selection is the only nonrandom cause of evolution.

Explore ONLINE!

This horned lizard has poisonous, foul smelling blood that it squirts out of its eyes as a defense against predators.

© Houghton Mifflin Harcourt • Image Credits: (t) ©Byron Jorjorian/Alamy; (b) ©Raymond Mendez/Animals Animals/Earth Scenes

Model Natural Selection in a Population

You will model natural selection in a population. You will analyze your data to draw conclusions about the environment's role in determining which traits help individuals to survive and reproduce.

MATERIALS
- colored pencils
- construction paper, 3 different colors
- hole punch
- paper or fabric, patterned
- stopwatch

Procedure

STEP 1 Use a hole punch to make 20 dots of each paper color to represent the prey population. The starting prey population equals 60 individuals. Also make some extra dots of each color to use as offspring.

STEP 2 As two group members (the predators) look away, have a third group member (the gamekeeper) scatter the prey on the patterned paper or fabric.

STEP 3 When your teacher says "start," the predators turn to face the habitat. They have 10 seconds to remove as many prey individuals from the habitat as they can, one at a time, using only one hand. The predators must stop picking up prey when your teacher says "stop."

STEP 4 To simulate reproduction, add one dot of the same color for each prey that survived "predation" in the habitat. Record the next-generation numbers for each color of prey in the data table.

| Generation | Number of Individuals | | |
	Color 1:	Color 2:	Color 3:
1st	20	20	20
2nd			
3rd			

STEP 5 Repeat Steps 3–4 to complete a third generation.

STEP 6 Make a graph plotting the number of surviving prey individuals for each color over three generations. Use colored pencils that match the construction paper dots.

© Houghton Mifflin Harcourt

Analysis

STEP 7 Describe any patterns in the prey population between the first and third generation. Provide an explanation for this pattern.

STEP 8 What effect did capturing an individual of a particular color have on the number of individuals of that color in the following generation?

STEP 9 If the habitat remained the same, predict how the variation in body color trait would change through three more generations.

STEP 10 Why might changing the habitat cause prey individuals of different colors to survive better through three generations?

EVIDENCE NOTEBOOK

10. What environmental factors might make a strong odor an advantage for the rafflesia? Record your evidence.

Evolution by Natural Selection

Owls are birds of prey that hunt other animals for food. The great horned owl can be found in many habitats between the Arctic and South America. These owls are named for tufts of feathers on their heads that look like horns. A wide wingspan, powerful talons, and keen eyesight make these owls powerful hunters. Evolution by natural selection over many millions of years resulted in these adaptations. In order for natural selection to occur, certain conditions must be present in a population.

Great horned owls can catch large prey, such as other birds. They also eat small rodents, frogs, and scorpions.

Variation in Traits

During sexual reproduction, alleles present in each parent separate into different eggs and sperm. Each chick receives a unique combination of alleles, resulting in genetic variation in the owl population. Random mutations can also add new alleles to the population. Adaptation is possible when genetic variation provides a variety of traits in the population. Some of these traits may increase a chick's chance of surviving and reproducing.

There are genetic differences between young owls in the same clutch.

11. **Discuss** Brainstorm a list of traits for which there might be genetic variation in this clutch of owls.

© Houghton Mifflin Harcourt • Image Credits: (t) ©Noella Ballenger/Alamy; (b) ©Design Pics Inc./Richard Wear/Alamy Images

Inheritance of Variation

Great horned owl offspring inherit different traits from their parents. For example, some owl chicks may inherit traits that provide advantages in the environment, such as longer talons or sharper eyesight. Others may receive less beneficial traits, such as weaker wing muscles or low birth weight. Chicks that survive and reproduce will pass traits to their own offspring.

12. Variation in great horned owl body size due to food supply *can / cannot* be acted on by natural selection. Variation in body size due to inherited traits *can / cannot* be acted on by natural selection.

Nearly 30 pounds of force is needed to open the talons of a great horned owl. Captured prey have little chance of escape.

Differential Survival

A population's environment determines which traits allow for a better chance of survival and reproductive success. Over many generations, traits that help an organism survive in the environment tend to add up in a population. Owls with longer talons or sharper vision are best able to grab moles or lizards from field grasses and forest shrubs. These well-fed owls survive and pass on their genes to the next generation. As the natural selection process continues through each generation, more and more owls inherit helpful traits.

13. Most birds have feathers that make "whooshing" sounds when they fly. Owls have feathers that result in near-silent flight, allowing them to sneak up on prey. Explain how natural selection led to this adaptation for owls.

© Houghton Mifflin Harcourt • Image Credits: (t) ©Matthew Cuda/Alamy; (b) ©Jill Lang/Fotolia

14. When an environmental change is extreme and rapid, populations may be
less / more likely to adapt because the process of natural selection occurs over
one / many generation(s). In these cases, populations may be less / more
likely to become extinct.

Engineer It
Control Selection to Meet Human Needs

Scientists can use their understanding about how the natural world works to engineer
solutions to problems. For example, understanding the process of natural selection
allows scientists and farmers to work together to produce healthy, plentiful crops for
the rapidly growing human population. They can identify beneficial plant traits and
control reproduction so that these traits are passed on to offspring. This is called *artificial
selection* because people, not nature, are selecting desired traits.

15. One source of groundwater
pollution is pesticide runoff
from crop fields. How could
artificial selection be used to
address this problem?

A. Farmers select plants
that are most resistant to
pests, which reduces the
need for pesticides.

B. Farmers select plants
that are least resistant to
pests, which increases
the need for pesticides.

C. The environment selects
plants that are most
resistant to pests, which
reduces the need for
pesticides.

Using artificial selection to improve plant resistance to pests can greatly increase
crop yields.

D. The environment selects plants that are least resistant to pests, which increases
the need for pesticdes.

16. How is artificial selection similar to natural selection? How is it different?

_____

_____

_____

_____

_____

_____

© Houghton Mifflin Harcourt • Image Credits: ©Artville/Getty Image

Analyzing Patterns of Natural Selection

Hammerhead sharks are predators that can often be found prowling reefs in shallow ocean waters. They eat a variety of prey including fish, octopus, and crabs. Scientists have made hypotheses about the unusual head shape of these sharks. Research suggests that the wide-spaced eyes improve the shark's vision. Improved vision may help the shark better track fast-moving prey. Researchers have also hypothesized that the head shape may help the shark dive and perform movements needed to catch its favorite meal—stingrays. The shark uses its wide, flat head to pin down stingrays that are hiding under the sand on the ocean floor.

Hammerhead sharks are named for their unusual head shape.

17. Discuss Choose one of the hypotheses about the function of the shark's head shape. Describe how a scientist might design an experiment to test the hypothesis.

18. Discuss Researchers have discovered that the wide-set eyes result in a large blind spot directly in front of the shark's head. How is it possible that this head shape evolved given this disadvantage?

Patterns of Natural Selection

Natural selection is a process that can be observed, measured, and tested. Data has been gathered from the field and the laboratory by thousands of scientists. These data document the evolution of populations in response to changes in their environment. For example, the increase in antibiotic-resistant bacteria, pesticide-resistant insects, and herbicide-resistant plants show that these organisms are changing by the process of natural selection. Scientists have also measured changes in the timing of animal migrations and flowering of plants in response to changes in climate. The patterns observed in these data can help scientists explain how populations may have changed in the past. They can also be used to predict how populations might change in the future.

© Houghton Mifflin Harcourt • Image Credits: ©frantisek hojdysz/Fotolia

Case Study: Body Size in Male Salmon

The graph below shows a pattern of selection in male coho salmon. The red dotted line shows a normal distribution for the trait. Most males have a medium body size. The blue line shows the distribution after selection has occurred.

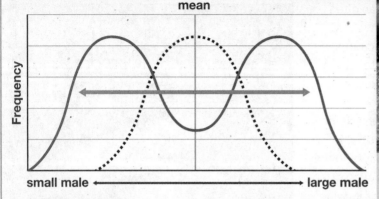

Male salmon, such as this coho salmon, defend territory.

19. Large male salmon defend territory and keep other males away from females. Small males can often sneak into a territory, unseen by the large male. How might this explain the pattern shown in the graph?

Case Study: Coat Color in Polar Bears

Genetic evidence reveals that polar bears are most closely related to a species of brown bear living on Alaska's ABC islands. Brown bears show a range of coat colors from solid brown to brown with light spots. The graph shows the selection pattern for coat color that occurred in polar bears.

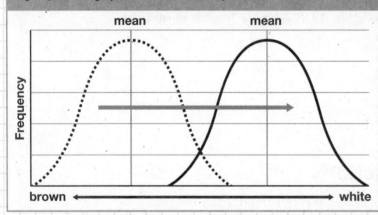

Polar bears spend much of their time on sea ice hunting for seals.

20. Polar bears have coats that help them survive in the cold Arctic where they live. The color of the coat helps them to blend in with their environment. The specialized hair cells that make up the coat keep the bear warm and dry. It is likely that *one/more than one* environmental factor caused the evolution of *one/more than one* trait in the polar bear.

© Houghton Mifflin Harcourt • Image Credits: (t) ©Gary Vestal/Photographer's Choice/Getty Images; (b) ©Andrew Watson/Fotolia

Case Study: Spine Number in Cacti

A population of desert cacti shows variation in the number of spines on the cactus surface. A new predator species migrates to the cactus habitat that prefers to eat cacti that have low spine numbers. Cactus individuals with high spine numbers are likely to have more parasites that lay their eggs at the base of the spines.

Cactus spines are a limited defense against predators. Predator populations also evolve adaptive traits because of natural selection.

21. Draw Create a distribution graph of the spine-number trait for the cactus population based on the information provided.

Frequency (vertical axis)

Number of spines (horizontal axis)

22. Language SmArts Write an explanation of the selection pattern shown in your graph. Explain how changes in the cacti's environment resulted in changes in the cactus population's trait.

EVIDENCE NOTEBOOK

23. How would you expect the distribution of traits for odor strength in rafflesia to change over many generations? Record your evidence.

© Houghton Mifflin Harcourt • Image Credits: ©GoneWithTheWind/Fotolia

Analyzing Natural Selection in Medium Ground Finches

In studies conducted on one of the Galápagos Islands, scientists observed the effect of natural events on the beak shape of a population of medium ground finches. They measured the size and shape of the beaks of thousands of finches on the island.

Medium ground finches usually eat small, soft seeds that are plentiful on the island. During a drought in 1977, plants on the island did not produce many seeds. The soft seeds were quickly eaten up. Finches that could eat larger, harder seeds instead of small, soft seeds were able to survive. Finches that could not eat the larger seeds died of starvation. Researchers compared measurements of average beak size before and after the drought.

24. Create a bar graph that shows the average beak measurements before and after the drought.

Average Beak Size in Medium Ground Finches		
	1977 (before drought)	**1978 (after drought)**
beak length (mm)	10.68	11.07
beak depth (mm)	9.42	9.96
beak width (mm)	8.68	9.01

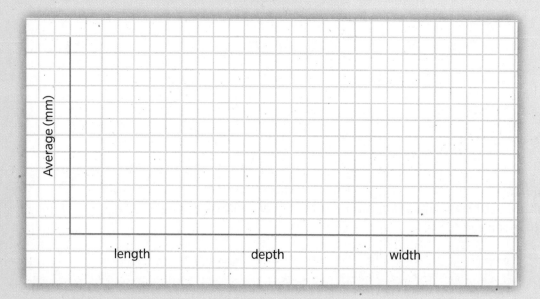

25. Use the graph and the text to describe how the drought resulted in the selection pattern shown in the ground finches.

_____

_____

_____

_____

© Houghton Mifflin Harcourt • Image Credits: ©Sylvain Cordier/Science Source

Continue Your Exploration

Name: _____ / Date: _____

Check out the path below or go online to choose one of the other paths shown.

Evolution of Drug-Resistant Bacteria

- **Hands-On Labs** 👋
- **Early Ideas about Evolution**
- **Propose Your Own Path**

Go online to choose one of these other paths.

A bacterial cell may have an allele that results in resistance to an antibiotic medicine. This cell may survive antibiotic treatment and pass the beneficial allele to its offspring. Scientists identified bacterial strains resistant to penicillin within 20 years of the first use of the antibiotic in humans. Bacterial resistance to levofloxacin, an antibiotic used to treat pneumonia and other life-threatening infections, developed within just one year. Scientists observed two contrasting trends. The number of antibiotic-resistant bacteria was increasing, while the development of new antibiotic medicines was decreasing.

1. What is needed for a population of bacteria to develop resistance to antibiotics? Select all that apply.

   A. genetic variation

   B. the presence of antibiotics in the bacteria's environment

   C. competition between bacterial species

   D. transfer of alleles from parent to offspring

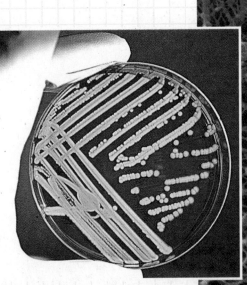

"Superbugs," like *Klebsiella pneumoniae*, the bacteria growing on the petri dish, resist almost all antibiotics. The colored micrograph (right) shows the bacterium trapped by a white blood cell.

© Houghton Mifflin Harcourt • Image Credits: (r) ©Science Photo Library/Getty Images; (l) ©Scharvik/iStock/Getty Images Plus/Getty Images

Continue Your Exploration

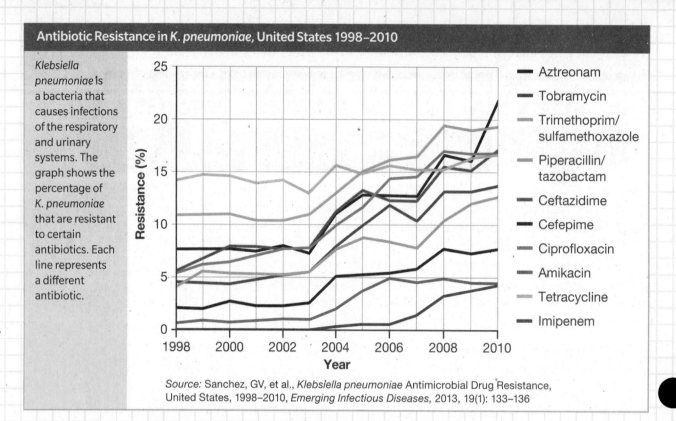

Antibiotic Resistance in *K. pneumoniae*, United States 1998–2010

Klebsiella pneumoniae is a bacteria that causes infections of the respiratory and urinary systems. The graph shows the percentage of *K. pneumoniae* that are resistant to certain antibiotics. Each line represents a different antibiotic.

- Aztreonam
- Tobramycin
- Trimethoprim/ sulfamethoxazole
- Piperacillin/ tazobactam
- Ceftazidime
- Cefepime
- Ciprofloxacin
- Amikacin
- Tetracycline
- Imipenem

Source: Sanchez, GV, et al., *Klebsiella pneumoniae* Antimicrobial Drug Resistance, United States, 1998–2010, *Emerging Infectious Diseases*, 2013, 19(1): 133–136

2. Describe the pattern of antibiotic resistance shown in the graph. What does the percentage of resistance at the beginning of the study tell you about each antibiotic?

3. These bacteria reproduce rapidly, doubling their population in only 40 minutes. How do you think this affects the frequency of alleles for antibiotic resistance?

4. **Collaborate** Work with a classmate to research other examples of natural selection that have been observed and measured by scientists. Prepare an oral presentation or short play for each example. Identify the variation of traits in the population, describe the environmental change, and explain why certain traits are increasing or decreasing in the population due to natural selection.

© Houghton Mifflin Harcourt

Can You Explain It?

Name: _____   Date: _____

How has the smell of rotting flesh become an adaptation for the rafflesia flower?

EVIDENCE NOTEBOOK

Refer to the notes in your Evidence Notebook to help you construct an explanation for how the adaptations of the rafflesia flower are related to the process of natural selection.

1. State your claim. Make sure your claim fully explains how the smell of rotting flesh became an adaptation for the rafflesia flower.

2. Summarize the evidence you have gathered to support your claim and explain your reasoning.

© Houghton Mifflin Harcourt • Image Credits: ©Fadil Aziz/Corbis Documentary/Getty Images

Checkpoints

Answer the following questions to check your understanding of the lesson.

Use the table to answer Questions 3–4.

3. Which statements could be true based on the data shown in the table? Select all that apply.

   A. The *B* allele does not provide a survival advantage to the population.

   B. This population is evolving.

   C. The *b* allele does not provide a survival advantage to the population.

   D. The population is not evolving.

Generation	Allele Frequency of *B*	Allele Frequency of *b*
1	0.63	0.37
2	0.71	0.29
3	0.78	0.22
4	0.78	0.22
5	0.81	0.19

4. How might the migration of individuals in or out of the habitat affect the frequency of each allele in this population?

   A. Migration will change the frequency of only the *B* allele.

   B. Migration will not change the frequency of either allele.

   C. Migration will change the frequency of both alleles.

   D. Migration will change the frequency of only the *b* allele.

Use the photo to answer Question 5.

5. Which environmental factors might cause a decrease in the size of hooks in the fish hook ant population over time? Select all that apply.

   A. Birds prefer to eat ants with smaller hooks.

   B. Ants with smaller hooks need less food to survive.

   C. Female ants prefer mates with smaller hooks.

   D. Small snakes cannot swallow ants with long hooks.

The fish hook ant has razor-sharp hooks to defend itself from predators.

© Houghton Mifflin Harcourt • Image Credits: ©Noppharat05081977/iStock/Getty Images Plus/Getty Images

---

6. Many species produce more offspring than can survive in their environment. How might this contribute to natural selection? Select all that apply.

   A. More offspring results in more competition for resources.

   B. Producing many offspring is a disadvantage.

   C. Helpful traits allow some individuals to outcompete others.

   D. Without competition, advantageous traits may have no effect on survival or reproduction.

Interactive Review

Complete this section to review the main concepts of the lesson.

Genetic variation of traits is necessary for a population to evolve, or change over time.

A. Explain how genetic variation and the environment influence the distribution of traits.

Natural selection is a process by which a population's environment determines which traits are beneficial and which are not.

B. Describe the three factors required for natural selection to occur in a population.

Populations become better adapted to their current environments through natural selection.

C. Explain why adaptations are specific to the current environment of a population.

© Houghton Mifflin Harcourt • Image Credits: (t) ©robert cicchetti/Shutterstock; (c) ©Design Pics Inc./Richard Wear/Alamy Images; (b) ©frantisek hojdysz/Fotolia

Speciation and Extinction

There are over 360,000 documented species of beetles, making them the most species-rich group of organisms on Earth.

By the end of this lesson . . .

you will be able to explain causes of speciation and extinction.

© Houghton Mifflin Harcourt • Image Credits: ©pixelprof/iStock/Getty Images Plus/ Getty Images

CAN YOU EXPLAIN IT?

Why did the number of mammal species on Earth suddenly explode over a relatively short period of time?

Millions of Years Ago

200	144	65	23	0
Jurassic	Cretaceous	Paleogene	Neogene	

Monotremata

Marsupialia

Xenarthra

Afrotheria

Lagomorpha

Rodentia

Scandentia

Primates

Eulipotyphla

Cetartiodactyla

Chiroptera

Perissodactyla

Carnivora

Source: The changing face of the molecular evolutionary clock, Ho, Simon Y.W.
Trends in Ecology & Evolution, Volume 29, Issue 9, 496 - 503

This diagram is a visual representation of how scientists think groups of mammals evolved over time. It is based on evidence from the fossil record, physical similarities, and genetic data.

1. Compare the number of mammal groups that existed 200 million years ago to the number that exist today. What do you think could have caused this change?

© Houghton Mifflin Harcourt

EVIDENCE NOTEBOOK As you explore the lesson, gather evidence to help explain factors that led to the rapid speciation of mammals on Earth.

Explaining Speciation

The Ming Dynasty completed construction of the Great Wall of China nearly 600 years ago. Today, populations of wind-pollinated plants that grow on different sides of the wall share more genes than populations of insect-pollinated plants that grow on different sides of the wall.

The Great Wall of China is a barrier between plant populations.

2. **Discuss** Describe how you think the Great Wall affects the reproduction of plant species pollinated by insects compared with plant species pollinated by wind.

Species and Speciation

A **species** is a group of individuals that can reproduce successfully in nature. This is a useful definition, but an imperfect one. For example, it is difficult to apply to organisms that reproduce asexually. Even so, the species concept is very useful as a scientific model. It is a testable idea that scientists can use to explain natural events.

Scientists apply the species concept to study how new species form. **Speciation** occurs when two or more populations no longer successfully reproduce. Speciation requires a barrier to reproduction, which stops the flow of genes between populations.

3. The speciation process can begin if different populations start to specialize in different food resources or habitats. Compare the beaks of the two honeycreepers shown in the photos. Which bird do you think eats seeds? Which bird do you think eats nectar?

The i'iwi, a Hawaiian honeycreeper, lives at high elevations on the islands of Hawai'i, Maui, and Kaua'i.

The palila, another species of Hawaiian honeycreeper, lives only on the west side of Mauna Kea, a Hawai'i volcano.

© Houghton Mifflin Harcourt • Image Credits: (t) ©wusuowei/Fotolia; (c) ©Photo Resource Hawaii/Alamy; (b) ©Gordon & Cathy Illg/Jaynes Gallery/Danita Delimont/Alamy

Causes of Speciation

For speciation to occur, populations must be *reproductively isolated*, which means they are unable to reproduce with each other. Geographic barriers, such as the formation of mountains or a river, are one cause of reproductive isolation. Isolation between two populations may also occur if individuals begin to specialize in different food sources or habitats, or develop different behaviors related to mating. The lemurs of Madagascar are an example of speciation. There are several hypotheses about how the ancestor species of the lemurs arrived on the island. For example, the ancestor species may have floated to Madagascar from Africa or traveled on a now-extinct land bridge. Speciation of this ancestor resulted in the more than 50 lemur species now living on the island.

Case Study: Speciation of Lemurs

This map shows elevation and rivers in Madagascar, an island off the southeast coast of Africa. Winds bring rain clouds to the island's eastern coast, but they lose all their moisture crossing the central mountains. This pattern creates different climate zones.

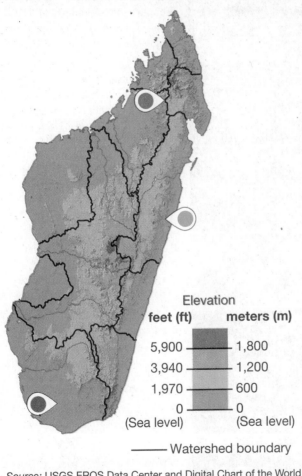

Elevation

feet (ft)	meters (m)
5,900	1,800
3,940	1,200
1,970	600
0 (Sea level)	0 (Sea level)

—— Watershed boundary

Source: USGS EROS Data Center and Digital Chart of the World (ESRI), as quoted by Center for Conservation Biology, Stanford University

Common brown lemurs live mostly in the dry forests of northwestern Madagascar. They mainly eat fruits, young leaves, and flowers.

Red-bellied lemurs live in the moist, lowland forests of eastern Madagascar. They eat the flowers, leaves, and fruit of over 67 plant species.

Ring-tailed lemurs eat whatever they can find in the sparse vegetation of southern Madagascar, including fruit, leaves, flowers, bark, sap, and sometimes insects.

4. Lemur populations on Madagascar may have become reproductively isolated by different mating behaviors / geographic barriers. Madagascar has several different climate zones, so lemur populations may also have become isolated because of similarities / differences in habitat use.

© Houghton Mifflin Harcourt • Image Credits: (t) ©J & C Sohns/Picture Press/Getty Images; (c) ©rybalov77/iStock/Getty Images Plus/Getty Images; (b) ©mdennah/Fotolia

Hands-On Lab
Analyze Speciation of Salamanders

Use habitat comparisons and a map to analyze the distribution of a group of closely related California salamanders. Use your analysis to write an explanation about how speciation may have occurred from a single ancestral species.

MATERIALS
- colored pencils
- index cards

Procedure and Analysis

STEP 1 Read the information about each salamander and its habitat. Make your own salamander card for each salamander.

STEP 2 Study the map on the next page, showing the distribution of these salamander species. Notice that the Central Valley forms a barrier between certain species. Identify which species live on each side of the valley.

STEP 3 Describe any patterns in physical appearance and habitat with the species on each side of the Central Valley.

Habitats of Ensatina Salamanders in California

E.e. xanthoptica live in coastal mountain ranges, often hiding under moist logs within coastal forests. The region has a Mediterranean climate.

E.e. platensis live in the inland forests of the Sierra Nevada mountains. Patterned skin helps them hide from predators during the dry summers.

E.e. oregonensis live in coastal mountain ranges and northern forests. They find ample hiding places within the damp forests of the north.

E.e. eschscholtzii live in coastal mountain ranges. They forage for worms and centipedes within the moist soil of coastal forests.

E.e. klauberi live in inland forests of the southern coastal mountain range. Closest to the Mojave Desert, they seek shelter from hawks within lakeside forests.

E.e. croceater live in dry forests of the southern coastal mountain range. With few shrubs for cover, yellow patterning helps them hide on lichen-patched trees.

E.e. picta occurs in a small range along the Pacific coast in northwest California. Its coloring helps it blend in with logs and leaves it lives in on the forest floor.

© Houghton Mifflin Harcourt • Image Credits: (1, 2, 4, 6) ©Chuck Brown/Science Source; (3) ©Dante Fenolio/Science Source; (5) ©James Hanken/Photoshot;

Distribution of Six Salamander Species in California

Central Valley

PACIFIC OCEAN

CA

N
W — E
S

E.e. oregonensis
E.e. picta
E.e. platensis
E.e. xanthoptica
E.e. croceater
E.e. eschscholtzii
E.e. klauberi

Source: Nafis, G., 2000–2016, A Guide to the Amphibians and Reptiles of California, http://www.californiaherps.com

STEP 4 Use the salamander cards to model how speciation may have occurred from a single ancestral species, as populations spread around California's long Central Valley. Describe your model as a sequence of steps that account for how each species could have become reproductively isolated.

STEP 5 Compare your sequence from Step 4 with the sequence of another classmate or group. Do you have similar evolution stories? Describe any differences.

STEP 6 The ranges of solid-colored and patterned salamanders overlap at the southern end of California's Central Valley. Scientists wonder if *E.e. klauberi* and *E.e.eschscholtzii* are the same species. To find out, scientists should determine if individuals from these two populations choose to share food resources / mate with each other in nature.

EVIDENCE NOTEBOOK

5. How might the speciation of California salamanders relate to the speciation of mammals over time? Record your evidence.

© Houghton Mifflin Harcourt

Analyze Soapberry Bug Evolution

Soapberry bugs occupy the tropical and temperate habitats of many continents, where soapberry plants thrive. Soapberry bugs feed on the seeds contained inside the fruits of soapberry plants. They use a beak-like structure to pierce the fruit and get to the seed. Then they use their beak to pierce the seed, inject digestive juices into the seed, and suck up the digested seed matter.

The red-shouldered bug is a type of soapberry bug found in southern Florida. It feeds on a native soapberry plant, the balloon vine, which has large, round fruits. In the 1950s, a new species of soapberry plant, the golden rain tree, was introduced to Florida. This plant produces fruit that is flat and thin. Researchers observed changes in the beak length of the bugs in response to the new plant over only a few decades.

This red-shouldered bug is one of many species of soapberry bugs.

6. Analyze the graph that shows the size ranges in beak length in populations of red-shouldered bugs that feed on balloon vine fruit compared with populations that feed on golden rain tree fruit. Write an explanation that describes the effect of the introduction of the golden rain tree on the evolution of the red-shouldered bug. Use evidence from the text to support your explanation.

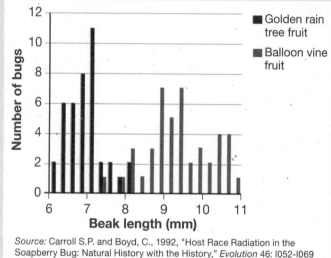

Source: Carroll S.P. and Boyd, C., 1992, "Host Race Radiation in the Soapberry Bug: Natural History with the History," *Evolution* 46: I052-I069

_____

_____

_____

_____

_____

_____

_____

7. Is it possible to predict with certainty if these two populations will become two species in the future? Why or why not?

_____

_____

_____

_____

_____

_____

_____

© Houghton Mifflin Harcourt • Image Credits: ©Caldwell Elusive Nature/Alamy

Explaining Extinction

Two hundred fifty million years ago, volcanic eruptions and other global changes caused the death of nearly 70% of all land species and 95% of all marine species on Earth. Though alarming, the "Great Dying" left openings in the environment that allowed surviving populations to move into new habitats. Devastation of seedless plant forests was followed by the rise of seed plants. The loss of many animals left openings for surviving reptiles, leading to the age of dinosaurs.

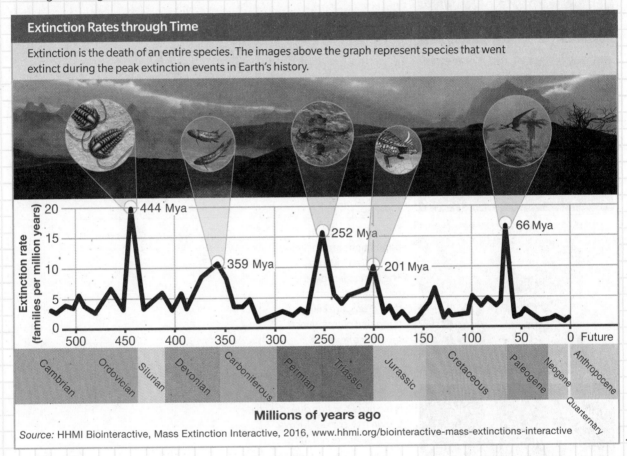

Extinction Rates through Time

Extinction is the death of an entire species. The images above the graph represent species that went extinct during the peak extinction events in Earth's history.

Source: HHMI Biointeractive, Mass Extinction Interactive, 2016, www.hhmi.org/biointeractive-mass-extinctions-interactive

8. **Discuss** Describe the pattern shown in the graph.

Extinction

Ninety-nine percent of species that have ever lived are now extinct. **Extinction** occurs when there are no members of a species left on Earth. *Background extinctions* happen at a fairly constant rate as species fail to adapt or compete in their environments while others succeed. At certain points in history, however, large changes to Earth's environment have caused *mass extinctions,* in which more than 50% of existing species went extinct within a few million years. Causes of mass extinctions include asteroid collisions, rapid changes to sea level, or geological events, such as earthquakes or volcanic eruptions.

The Panamanian golden frog is bred in captivity by conservationists but may be extinct in its natural habitat. The frog was last seen in the wild in 2009.

© Houghton Mifflin Harcourt • Image Credits: ©Naturbild/Superstock

9. Read the information about each *endangered species*—species at risk of extinction. Then use the factors listed in the word bank to describe the extinction threat for each species.

- climate change
- habitat loss
- competition
- pollution
- predation

red panda

Red pandas are in danger of extinction due to the spread of agricultural activities, including deforestation. The pandas live only in the Himalayan mountains of Nepal and China.

Extinction threat:

white bark pine

As average temperatures rise, tree-boring beetles can spread to higher elevations and infest more and more white bark pines.

Extinction threat:

monarch butterfly

Migrating monarch populations are declining due to pesticide use. The pesticides, used by farmers to protect their crops, are killing milkweed plants where monarchs lay eggs.

Extinction threat:

mariana fruit bat

Guam's Mariana fruit bat is facing extinction due to brown tree snakes. Brown tree snakes are not native to Guam. They frequently eat small mammals, such as bats.

Extinction threat:

red squirrel

Gray squirrels are not native to Great Britain. They have been introduced there, driving native red squirrels away. The gray squirrels are better foragers than the red squirrels.

Extinction threat:

Images; (c) ©Mark Herreid/Shutterstock; (bc) ©Merlin D. Tuttle/Science Source; (b) ©Ben Queenborough/Oxford Scientific/Getty Images

© Houghton Mifflin Harcourt • Image Credits: (t) ©MarieHolding/iStock/Getty Images Plus/Getty Images; (tc) ©Don Becker/USGS/Smith Collection/Gado/Archive Photos/Getty Plus/Getty Images

Human Activity and Extinction

Human activity is a relatively new cause of extinctions. While unintended, the way we interact with the environment to live, eat, produce energy, and build economies affects the health of ecosystems. Clearing of land for farms, cities, and roads causes loss of habitats. Overuse of plants and animals for food, medicine, shelter, and sport threatens many species. When the rate of use is faster than the rate of reproduction, a species may become extinct. Human activity is also linked to pollution, climate change, and the spread of invasive species. If human induced environmental changes are extreme or rapid, populations may not have time to adapt and survive.

The current rate of extinctions is more than 100 times the expected background rate. Scientists predict the loss of a large number of species over the next century. Conservation actions are increasing in an effort to keep pace.

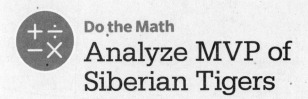

Do the Math

Analyze MVP of Siberian Tigers

To determine if a species is facing possible extinction and to plan conservation efforts, scientists calculate a *minimum viable population* (MVP). The MVP is the smallest number of individuals needed for a population to survive for more than 40 generations given current environmental conditions.

The Russian Siberian tiger population dropped to only 40 individuals in the 1940s. The Russian government passed protection laws, and now the population remains steady at about 540 individuals. Conservationists estimate that 5,000 tigers are needed to meet the MVP. Over the course of one generation, which averages 12.5 years in tigers, 170 tigers will be lost to poaching, road deaths, and natural causes in Russia's Siberian tiger population.

10. How many tigers die each year?

11. How many tiger cubs must be born each year for the population to remain at 540 individuals? Hint: deaths=births when a population size remains steady.

12. Assuming the death rate remains constant, how many cubs must be born each year to reach the tiger's MVP of 5,000 tigers in two generations, or 25 years?

© Houghton Mifflin Harcourt • Image Credits: ©Frank Pali/All Canada Photos/Getty Images

EVIDENCE NOTEBOOK

13. Sixty-six million years ago, a mass extinction called the KPg extinction wiped out about 75% of all plant and animal species on Earth, including all flightless dinosaurs. How might this mass extinction have allowed for the rise of mammal species? Record your evidence.

Engineer It

Identify Solutions for a Wildlife Corridor

The Canadian lynx is a threatened species. Logging, oil drilling, land development, and winter recreation break up the lynx habitat. Fires, including controlled burns, reduce the habitat of snowshoe hares, a common food source for the lynx. For lynx to rebound and succeed, they need a large, continuous range. Conservationists look for solutions that give the lynx free range and good hunting grounds from Canada into the United States. Solutions must also meet human needs for industry, transportation, agriculture, and recreation. The map shows protected areas inside the wildlife corridor area needed for a continuous lynx range.

Source: Laliberte, Andrea s., and William J. Ripple, 2004, "Range Contractions of North American Carnivores and Ungulates," BioScience, Vol. 54, Issue 2, 123–138.

14. What are the criteria and constraints associated with designing solutions for lynx habitat fragmentation and population decline?

_____

_____

_____

_____

_____

15. Match each numbered design solution with the location below where it would be used to help maintain a wildlife corridor for the lynx.

Design Solutions
1 Land bridge or tunnel
2 Wildlife-friendly fencing
3 No burn zones
4 Undeveloped "buffer" areas

____ housing communities and recreation areas within the corridor

____ land dedicated to farms and cattle ranches within the wildlife corridor

____ forested areas in Yellowstone National Park where lynx hunt for snowshoe hares

____ an interstate highway that crosses the corridor

© Houghton Mifflin Harcourt

Continue Your Exploration

Name: _____   **Date:** _____

Check out the path below or go online to choose one of the other paths shown.

People in Science

- **Hands-on Labs** ✋
- **Endangered Species**
- **Propose Your Own Path**

Go online to choose one of these other paths.

Dr. Nancy Knowlton, Marine Biologist

Nancy Knowlton fell in love with marine life while wandering the ocean shore as a child. Her work studying shrimp speciation began in Jamaica, where she learned that the native shrimp population that scientists believed to be a single species actually included four species. Her work with shrimp continued along the Isthmus of Panama—a narrow strip of land that separates the Atlantic and Pacific Oceans. There she studied how the formation of the isthmus contributed to the evolution of several shrimp species.

1. Imagine you were a member of Dr. Knowlton's team conducting research about shrimp species in the waters off Panama. What types of data would you need to collect to determine if the shrimp populations were separate species? What do you think a typical research day would be like?

Dr. Nancy Knowlton spent nearly 14 years studying the diversification of shrimp species along the Isthmus of Panama. She continues to dedicate her life to the conservation of coral reefs.

© Houghton Mifflin Harcourt • Image Credits: ©David Harp 1996

Continue Your Exploration

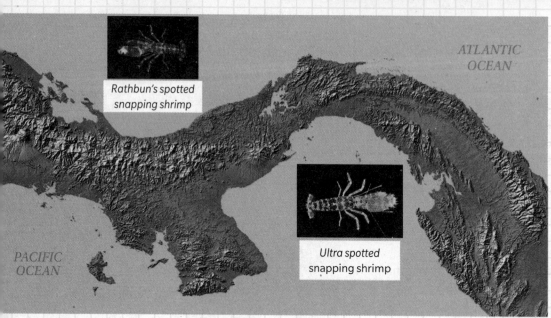

Rathbun's spotted snapping shrimp

ATLANTIC OCEAN

Ultra spotted snapping shrimp

PACIFIC OCEAN

The Isthmus of Panama is a narrow strip of land that connects North and South America and prevents the flow of water between the Atlantic and Pacific Oceans. Two shrimp species separated by the isthmus are shown on the map.

2. The movement of Earth's plates caused the formation of the Isthmus of Panama between 20 and 3.5 million years ago. Could the formation of the Isthmus of Panama alone cause a shrimp population to diversify into distinct species? Explain your reasoning.

3. To claim that the rise of the Isthmus of Panama contributed to shrimp speciation, would Dr. Knowlton need to establish that the east coast and west coast shrimp species diverged before or after the rise of the isthmus? Explain your reasoning.

4. **Collaborate** Rheas, emu, and ostrich are bird species that each live on different continents, but they are more closely related to each other than to nearby bird species. Work with a group to learn about their evolution from a common ancestor. Present your findings to your classmates. Include photos or drawings of each species in your report.

© Houghton Mifflin Harcourt • Image Credits: ©JPL/NIMA/SRTM/NASA

Can You Explain It?

Name: _____   **Date:** _____

Why did the number of mammal species on Earth suddenly explode over a relatively short period of time?

Millions of Years Ago

| 200 | 144 | 65 | 23 | 0 |

| Jurassic | Cretaceous | Paleogene | Neogene | |

Monotremata
Marsupialia
Xenarthra
Afrotheria
Lagomorpha
Rodentia
Scandentia
Primates
Eulipotyphla
Cetartiodactyla
Chiroptera
Perissodactyla
Carnivora

Source: The changing face of the molecular evolutionary clock, Ho, Simon Y.W. Trends in Ecology & Evolution, Volume 29, Issue 9, 496 - 503

EVIDENCE NOTEBOOK

Refer to the notes in your Evidence Notebook to help you construct an explanation for the rapid speciation of mammals on Earth.

1. State your claim. Make sure your claim fully explains factors that led to the rapid speciation of mammals on Earth.

2. Summarize the evidence you have gathered to support your claim and explain your reasoning.

© Houghton Mifflin Harcourt

Checkpoints

Answer the following questions to check your understanding of the lesson.

Use the photo to answer Questions 3 and 4.

3. The golden-cheeked warbler and the black-throated green warbler look nearly identical to each other. What type of information could be used to determine if the birds are separate species? Select all that apply.

A. The birds breed with each other where their territories overlap.

B. The birds show differences in mating songs and behaviors.

C. The birds do not breed with each other where their territories overlap.

D. The birds compete for food and nesting sites.

Bird watchers often mistake this black-throated green warbler for the rare golden-cheeked warbler.

4. Number the steps to show how the two warblers may have become different species.

____ The populations are exposed to different environmental factors.

____ The populations become reproductively isolated.

____ Ancestral populations are separated by a glacier.

____ Separated populations occupy different habitats.

Use the photo to answer Questions 5 and 6.

5. The most recent estimated population size for the Indus river dolphin population is 1,100 individuals. If the minimum viable population is much higher, what can you predict about the likelihood of the river dolphin's extinction?

A. Extinction of this species is not likely.

B. The dolphins are likely to go extinct within 40 generations.

C. The river dolphins will likely diversify into two species.

D. River dolphin conservation efforts are working.

The blind Indus river dolphin lives only in the shallows of the Indus River in Pakistan. The dolphin population fell sharply after the construction of dams along the river redirected water for crop irrigation.

6. Geologic events / human activities are a relatively recent cause of extinctions. The endangered status of the Indus river dolphin is the result of habitat destruction / pollution related to geologic events / human activities.

© Houghton Mifflin Harcourt • Image Credits: (t) ©George Grall/National Geographic Magazines/Getty Images; (b) ©Rizwan Tabassum/AFP/Getty Images

Interactive Review

Complete this section to review the main concepts of the lesson.

New species form when barriers to reproduction prevent gene flow between populations of organisms.

A. Describe factors that can lead to speciation.

Extinction occurs when there are no individuals of a species left on Earth.

B. Explain the cause-effect relationship between environmental changes and the extinction of species.

© Houghton Mifflin Harcourt • Image Credits: (t) ©wusuowei/Fot olia (b) ©MarieHolding/ iStock/Getty Images Plus/Getty Images

Choose one of the activities to explore how this unit connects to other topics.

☐ **Earth Science Connection**

Melting of Polar Ice Caps Climate change influences natural landforms as well as ecosystems and populations. The polar ice caps have been melting as global temperatures have increased, reducing the amount of ice and increasing sea levels.

Research the impacts of melting polar ice caps on a population of your choice. Based on the existing variation of traits in the population, predict how the changing environment might cause changes in the population. Use evidence from data to support your explanation. Create a poster or visual display that explains your prediction.

☐ **Art Connection**

Art and Extinction The purpose of extinction art is to raise awareness of endangered species, and species that have already become extinct. This branch of art can also help to relate human impacts on the environment to the risk of losing certain species.

Research an extinct species such as the Great auk, shown here, the Wake Island rail, the small Mauritian flying fox, the desert bandicoot, or the Round Island burrowing boa. Find out when and where the species lived and how it went extinct. Create a drawing of your species. Then summarize your research in a short paragraph.

☐ **Health Connection**

Evolutionary Medicine Evolutionary medicine uses knowledge of evolutionary biology to find different ways to prevent and treat certain diseases. Scientists investigate how diseases change over time in non-human animal species and then apply their findings to human health. For example, rhinoceroses can get leukemia, badgers can get tuberculosis, and some armadillos have leprosy.

Choose one of these examples to research. Find out what causes the disease, how the disease has changed over time, and how studying the non-human animal has increased our understanding. Organize your research into bullet points. Participate in a group discussion about how evolutionary medicine applies to the disease you have chosen.

© Houghton Mifflin Harcourt • Image Credits: (t) ©Peter J. Raymond/Science Source; (c) ©bilwissedition Ltd. & Co. KG/Alamy; (b) ©davemhuntphotography/iStock/Getty Images Plus/Getty Images

Name: _____   Date: _____

Complete this review to check your understanding of the unit.

Use the diagram to answer Questions 1–3.

1. What type of change is shown?

   A. adaptation

   B. extinction

   C. mutation

   D. protein folding

2. What type of changes would possibly result from the change in the new genetic sequence? Select all that apply.

   A. change in proteins

   B. change in traits

   C. change in behavior

   D. change in environmental conditions

3. If the genetic change results in a trait that is beneficial to the organism, that organism will be *more* / *less* likely to survive and reproduce than other organisms. If the trait continues to be beneficial in the organism's environment, that trait will likely *increase* / *decrease* in the population.

Genetic Change

original sequence

A A T G T G C C G
T T A C A C G G C

changed sequence

A G T G T G C C G
T C A C A C G G C

Use the photo of the brimstone butterfly to answer Questions 4–5.

4. How is leaf mimicry beneficial to this butterfly? Select all that apply.

   A. allows the butterfly to avoid predators

   B. allows the butterfly to access more food

   C. allows the butterfly to blend in with the leaves it rests on

   D. allows the butterfly to warn predators that it is poisonous and to avoid it

5. If the plant species that the brimstone butterfly mimics were to become extinct, what effects would this most likely have on the brimstone butterfly population? Select all that apply.

The brimstone leaf butterfly mimics a leaf to disguise itself from predators.

   A. Predators would see brimstone butterflies more easily.

   B. Brimstone butterflies would need to find another food source.

   C. Brimstone butterflies would change into a new species.

   D. Brimstone butterflies with wings that best blended in with plants remaining in the area would become more common in the population.

© Houghton Mifflin Harcourt • Image Credits: ©Christopher Grimmer/Shutterstock

6. Think about how each of these processes relates to evolution. Then complete the graphic organizer by identifying a cause, an effect, and an example of each process.

Process	Cause	Effect	Example
Genetic Mutation	Random changes in DNA		
Natural Selection			
Speciation			
Extinction			

© Houghton Mifflin Harcourt

Name: _____   Date: _____

Use the graph to answer Questions 7–10.

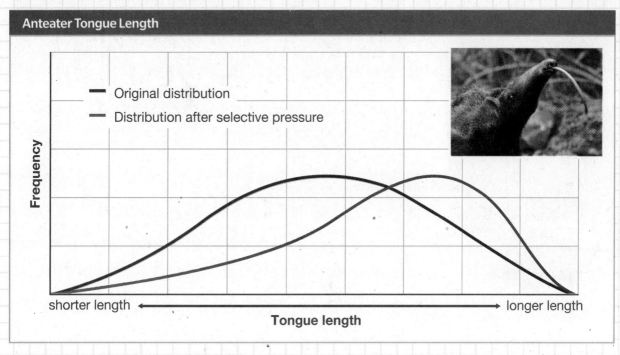

Anteater Tongue Length

— Original distribution
— Distribution after selective pressure

Frequency

shorter length ←————————————→ longer length

Tongue length

7. What variation of traits is shown in this graph?

8. Explain the connection between genes, proteins, and this variation of traits.

9. Compare and contrast the original distribution of traits prior to selective pressure to the most recent distribution.

10. An anteater's main food source is termites, which live underground. Propose an explanation for how selective pressure could have resulted in the change in traits within the anteater population shown in the graph.

© Houghton Mifflin Harcourt • Image Credits: ©Alexandre Fagundes De Fagundes/

Use the map to answer Questions 11–13.

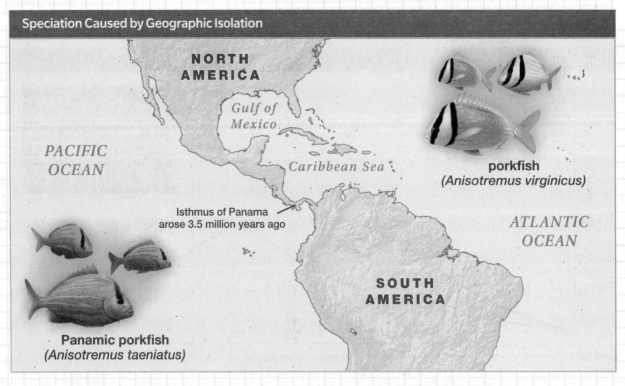

Speciation Caused by Geographic Isolation

NORTH AMERICA

Gulf of Mexico

PACIFIC OCEAN

Caribbean Sea

porkfish
(*Anisotremus virginicus*)

Isthmus of Panama
arose 3.5 million years ago

ATLANTIC OCEAN

SOUTH AMERICA

Panamic porkfish
(*Anisotremus taeniatus*)

11. Describe when and how the ancestor population of these two fish species became divided into two populations.

12. Even if the environmental conditions are similar for each population, why might the populations become different from each other over time?

13. If these two populations were no longer isolated, predict whether or not they would reproduce with each other.

© Houghton Mifflin Harcourt

Name: _____   Date: _____

How does the use of insecticides lead to insecticide resistance?

A single genetic mutation causes resistance to the insecticide DDT. This research is key to helping scientists improve malaria-control strategies related to mosquitoes. Research how certain insect species have become resistant to different insecticides over time. What types of variation exist in insect populations that have allowed insect populations to become resistant?

   Explain why it is important to minimize the use of harmful insecticides. Create a public education poster using the concept of natural selection to explain the issue of increasing insecticide resistance in insects.

Insecticide Resistance between 1940 and 1990

The number of insect species that are resistant to insecticides has changed over time. The different colors on this graph represent different groups of insecticides.

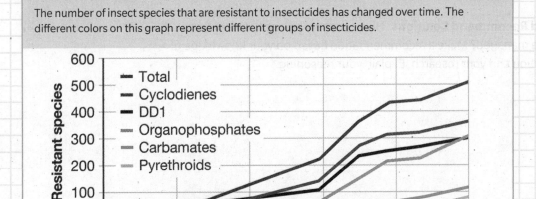

Source: Metcalfe, R.L., and W.H. Luckmann, eds., *Introduction to Insect Pest Management*, Third Edition, 1994, John Wiley and Sons, N.Y., as quoted by "DDT, Junk Science, Malaria, and insecticide resistance," Bug Gwen, Gwen Pearson, 2007

The steps below will help guide your research and develop your recommendation.

1. **Define the Problem** Write a statement defining the problem you have been asked to solve.

© Houghton Mifflin Harcourt

2. **Conduct Research** How have insects become resistant to insecticides over time?

3. **Analyze the Data** Use the graph to analyze how the resistance to insecticides has changed over time. Use the information to make predictions about how insecticide resistance might change in the future.

4. **Identify and Recommend Solutions** How can the incidence of insecticide resistance be managed? Make a recommendation based on your knowledge of natural selection and your research. Explain your reasoning.

5. **Communicate** Present your findings with a public education poster. Use the concept of natural selection to explain the issue of increasing insecticide resistance, and explain how your recommended solution would help address the problem.

✓ **Self-Check**

	I researched how insect species have become resistant to insecticides.
	I analyzed data to describe how resistance to insecticides has changed over time and to predict how it might change in the future.
	I used knowledge of natural selection to make a recommendation about how to manage insecticide resistance.
	My findings and recommendation were clearly communicated to others.

© Houghton Mifflin Harcourt

Human Influence on Inheritance

Africanized bees, sometimes called killer bees, are the result of breeding African honey bees with European honey bees to try to increase honey production.

© Houghton Mifflin Harcourt • Image Credits: ©Smithlandia Media/Moment/Getty Images

Humans have been influencing the traits of certain plants and animals for a very long time. For example, by carefully selecting seeds from specific plants, farmers began cultivating many of the delicious fruits, vegetables, and grains that we eat today. The selective breeding of crops was just the beginning of ways that humans can influence inheritance. Today we go even further by genetically modifying organisms to fit our needs and solve problems. In this unit, you will investigate how artificial selection and genetic engineering influence our lives.

Why It Matters

Here are some questions to consider as you work through the unit. Can you answer any of the questions now? Revisit these questions at the end of the unit to apply what you discover.

Questions	Notes
How has artificial selection resulted in dog and cat breeds that people enjoy as pets? How have these domesticated animals impacted society?	
What foods do you eat that have been modified through artificial selection?	
What types of design problems does the genetic modification of organisms address?	
How has the desire for improved traits driven technology related to genetic engineering?	
What are the environmental and ethical issues related to genetically modified organisms, including those that are food sources?	
Could genetically modified food sources affect human health?	

© Houghton Mifflin Harcourt

Unit Starter: Analyzing the Credibility of Sources

When conducting research, it is important to determine whether the information you find is from a reliable source. Some important questions to ask about these sources are: *Where was this research published? How does this information relate to what I already know? Who is behind the funding for this research?* Analyze this Internet search page to determine which of these pages are credible sources for scientific information.

genetically modified organisms

1. Getting the Facts about GMO :: Agency for the Protection of the Environment
www.ape.iep.org>Research and Education
Genetically Modified Organisms (GMO). What are GMOs? GMO is an acronym for genetically modified organisms...

2. Education about GMO–Institute of Science and Engineering
www.instituteofscienceandengineeringlearning.edu
Oct 2, 2016 – A GMO or genetically modified organism, is an organism that has been genetically altered or modified...

3. Learning Science–GMO
Ad www.synnagenes.com / e8654687%$64&*45
Quick answers to questions about GMO. Learn more...

4. Genetically modified organism – WikisInfo
http://www.ef.wikisinfo.org/info/aboutgmotech
A genetically modified organism has had its DNA genetically altered...

5. Genetically modified organism (GMO) – GMOs in medicine and science
http://www.usagricultural.gov
Agricultural plants are one of the most common genetically modified organisms...

6. What are Genetically Modified Organisms?
www.modifiedhealing_cclw.com > Blog Home > Wellness Articles
January 20, 2013 – Want to know about sprays used in genetically modified foods and seeds? A rapid...

1. Which sources likely provide the most credible scientific information about genetically modified organisms?

   A. sites 1, 2, and 3

   B. sites 4, 5, and 6

   C. sites 3, 5, and 6

   D. sites 1, 2, and 5

Go online to download the Unit Project Worksheet to help you plan your project.

Unit Project

Biotechnology and Crops

Humans have helped to develop many of the modern crop species we grow today, either through artificial selection, genetic modification, or a combination of both. Pick a food or fiber crop that humans have influenced genetically, and research the development of this crop over time. Explain how the development of this crop species has affected society.

© Houghton Mifflin Harcourt

Artificial Selection

Gardeners grow roses for their bright colors, fragrance, and soft petals. They grow the flowers in special ways to influence how often these traits show up in flower crops.

By the end of this lesson . . .

you will be able to explain how artificial selection influences the inheritance of traits in organisms.

© Houghton Mifflin Harcourt • Image Credits: ©Masamitsu/Fotolia

CAN YOU EXPLAIN IT?

How did humans cause alpacas to become different from vicuñas over time?

vicuña

alpaca

Vicuñas are shy, fast animals. They feed on short, tough grasses in the Andes Mountains. Alpacas are their relatives. They are gentle and curious. Alpacas are raised by humans for their warm wool.

1. Compare the way the alpaca and the vicuña look. How are they alike or different?

2. Do you think alpacas or vicuñas are more useful to humans? Explain your answer.

© Houghton Mifflin Harcourt • Image Credits: ©Heeb Christian/Prisma Bildagentur AG/Alamy; ©Paul Springett C/Alamy

EVIDENCE NOTEBOOK As you explore the lesson, gather evidence to help explain how humans influenced the development of alpaca populations from vicuñas.

Analyzing Human Influence on the Inheritance of Traits

Humans have been influencing the traits of certain plants and animals for thousands of years. For example, people may breed horses to race, or grow fruits that taste a certain way. People grow plants and keep animals for the products or services they provide. They separate these organisms from their wild populations. This affects the possible traits in the separated population. Over time, domesticated populations may become very different from their wild relatives.

People at the market may want to buy these tomatoes because of the colors and shapes.

3. **Discuss** What traits make each tomato type unique? Why might farmers want to grow tomatoes with so many different traits?

Traits Are Passed from Parents to Offspring

The Saint Bernard pass lies high in the Alps, a European mountain system. During the 1700s, a single monastery near the pass kept a population of large dogs with thick fur. The dogs helped the monks avoid avalanches and find people trapped in the snow. The monks depended on the dogs for survival. So, they bred only the most gentle and snow-wise dogs. Over time, these traits became common in the population of dogs. Even now, St. Bernard dogs will instinctively help people lying or trapped in the snow.

    The monks had little understanding of the biology behind inheritance. Yet, they knew that traits pass from parents to their young. They used this understanding to influence the dogs' traits through *selective breeding*, or the breeding of specific organisms based on preferred traits. More than 100 years later, scientists began to understand the way inheritance works.

© Houghton Mifflin Harcourt • Image Credits: ©funwithfood/E+/Getty Images

Scientific Understanding of Inheritance

Factors That Influence the Frequency of Traits Charles Darwin was an English naturalist who studied the inheritance of traits in living things. He loved raising pigeons. Darwin bred the birds to have certain features. He realized that nature, like humans, might influence the traits of living things. Darwin applied this thinking to data he collected from living and fossil organisms. He observed that traits that provide a benefit in a certain environment become more common in populations over time.

Inheritance Follows Patterns Gregor Mendel was an Austrian monk who studied traits in pea plants. He carefully bred peas. He learned that some traits follow a simple pattern when passed from parent to offspring. Dominant traits appear in offspring when present. Recessive traits might be present but masked. Mendel explained that there are two "factors" that can be inherited for each trait—one from each parent. These "factors" are now known as *alleles*. Modern genetics is based on Mendel's work.

Inheritance Patterns Can Be Predicted Reginald Punnett was a geneticist who built on Mendel's work. He studied more complex patterns of inheritance. Punnett developed a simple calculation table to predict the likelihood that offspring would inherit certain traits from parents. This table is called a *Punnett square*. Punnett used this table to show that certain feather colors in chickens are linked to being male.

© Houghton Mifflin Harcourt • Image Credits: ©Paul D. Stewart/Science Source; ©David Broadbent/Alamy; ©alphadogdesign/Fotolia

4. By observing inheritance patterns, Darwin, Mendel, and Punnett developed the foundation for understanding how breeding influences traits in a population. They worked before / after scientists understood the relationship between traits and genetic material. Society can use inheritance patterns to meet various needs because the patterns are unpredictable / predictable.

Hands-On Lab
Analyze Selected Traits in Vegetables

You will compare vegetable plants bred from wild cabbage, *Brassica oleracea*. You will analyze traits to describe how each vegetable could develop from wild cabbage by selective breeding.

Procedure and Analysis

STEP 1 Study the diagram of wild cabbage.

MATERIALS
- colored pencils
- samples of fresh vegetables cultivated from wild cabbage (*Brassica oleracea*), including broccoli, cauliflower, Brussels sprouts, kohlrabi, and kale

---

Anatomy of Wild Cabbage

Many types of vegetables were cultivated from wild cabbage plants. Some traits were encouraged and other traits were suppressed.

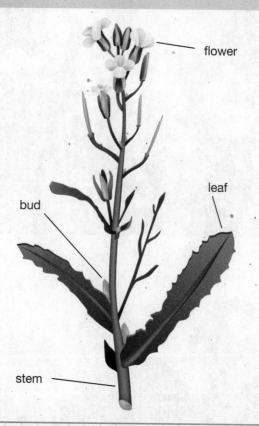

flower

leaf

bud

stem

STEP 2 Choose your first vegetable. Describe it in the table. Sketch the vegetable on a separate sheet of paper.

STEP 3 In your observations, circle specific traits the vegetable has in common with wild cabbage and note these in the table.

STEP 4 Repeat Steps 2 and 3 for each vegetable.

144 Unit 3 Human Influence on Inheritance

© Houghton Mifflin Harcourt

Vegetable	Observations

STEP 5 Which vegetables are the most and least similar to wild cabbage? What does this tell you about the selective breeding process for each vegetable?

STEP 6 Choose one of the vegetables from the table. Explain how it might have developed from wild cabbage through selective breeding.

Artificial Selection

The human control of reproduction in order to influence the traits present in offspring is called **artificial selection.** For example, dairy cows are bred for the amount of milk they produce, the milk fat level, and their pregnancy success. Artificial selection can encourage traits in a population that people want. It can also discourage traits that people do not want. Science can help describe the impact of artificial selection on populations. Society must then decide how to apply this knowledge.

The traits present in a population are different when humans are the selective pressure instead of environmental factors. The traits people choose may not improve an organism's chance for survival or reproduction. This is one way artificial selection is very different from natural selection. Yet, natural and artificial selection do follow some of the same rules. Both can only affect traits that are present in a population. Also, both selection types change the frequency of *phenotypes* (traits) and *genotypes* (gene combinations) in a population.

© Houghton Mifflin Harcourt

5. Which of these factors make dairy cows a good choice for artificial selection? Select all that apply.

    A. The cows vary in the amount of milk they make.

    B. The amount of milk cows make is affected by diet.

    C. The amount of milk cows make is an inherited trait.

    D. Many people want to drink milk or cook with milk.

 EVIDENCE NOTEBOOK

    6. What traits might have been selected for in alpacas? Record your evidence.

Predict the Outcome of Artificial Selection

Guppies are a popular fish for home aquariums. They have bright colors, broad tails, and spotted patterns. People who sell fish use selective breeding to emphasize certain traits in offspring. As a result, there are many types of guppies. For example, the half-black yellow guppy has a half-black body and a broad yellow tail. Every part of the albino red guppy is a striking scarlet color, even its eyes.

The color, spot pattern, shape, and size of guppies in a population can be influenced through artificial selection.

7. **Draw** Choose one trait of the guppies in the photo. Draw what a guppy might look like if people selected for this trait over ten generations. Include a caption that explains the process.

© Houghton Mifflin Harcourt • Image Credits: ©underworld11/iStock/Getty Images Plus/ Getty Images

Modeling the Genetic Basis for Artificial Selection

Humans raised dogs long before they farmed land or raised chickens and sheep. Dogs were the first animals bred by people, beginning between 10,000 and 40,000 years ago. Dogs are different from wolves because of selective breeding. Dogs have smaller skulls, paws, and teeth. Their ears flop forward. They are more friendly than fierce and can sense some human emotions.

8. How might humans have influenced the inheritance of traits they found desirable in wolves?

Wolves have traits that help them survive in the places they live.

Artificial Selection Acts on Heritable Traits

In the early 1900s, experiments confirmed Mendel's idea that traits are controlled by factors inherited from each parent. Over time, new technologies and discoveries linked traits to DNA. *DNA* is genetic material in cells that is transferred from parent to offspring during reproduction. *Genes* are segments of DNA that produce specific traits. As understanding of inheritance advances, so do the ways humans affect the traits in organisms.

Artificial selection makes traits that interest people more common in a population. Selective dog breeding can encourage obedience and a soft bite in some dogs.

9. A single gene determines if Chinese Shar-Peis will have a short and fluffy coat or a wrinkled coat. Two Shar-Peis that differ in coat type have different genotypes / phenotypes / genotypes and phenotypes. Breeding Shar-Peis so that they are more likely to have wrinkled skin is an example of natural / artificial selection. It requires traits that are / are not inherited from parents.

Dog breeders do not make new traits. Instead, they cause traits that dogs already have to become more or less common in a population. They do this by deciding which dogs mate. Puppies are more likely to have desired traits if both of their parents have those traits. Artificial selection directs change in populations that can occur more quickly than with natural selection. Artificial selection outcomes are also more predictable than those of natural selection because people control which individuals reproduce. Reproduction in nature may cause different traits to become more common in the population.

 EVIDENCE NOTEBOOK

10. How do artificial selection and heritable traits relate to the development of alpaca populations from vicuñas? Record your evidence.

© Houghton Mifflin Harcourt • Image Credits: ©Michael Cummings/Getty Images; ©carlos Restrepo/Fotolia

Model Artificial Selection

A *Punnett square* models the transfer of genes from parents to offspring during sexual reproduction. The gene versions (or *alleles*) for an inherited characteristic from one parent are listed above each column as letters. The alleles from the other parent are listed next to each row. Capital letters are used for dominant alleles. Lowercase letters are used for recessive alleles.

Genotype: *HH*
Phenotype: short hair

Genotype: *hh*
Phenotype: long hair

To complete the Punnett square, the parent alleles are combined in each cell. In this diagram, the allele for short hair, *H*, is dominant to the allele for long hair, *h*. Having at least one dominant allele will produce short hair, the dominant phenotype. The parent at the top has an *HH* genotype. The parent to the left has an *hh* genotype. In this example, the predicted ratio of short-haired dogs in a litter of four is 4:4. In other words, you could expect 100% of the dogs to have short hair.

11. A breeder crosses two *Hh* Chihuahuas. Complete the Punnett square that models this cross.

Short-haired Chihuahua

Short-haired Chihuahua

12. Based on the Punnett square modeling the cross of two *Hh* Chihuahuas, what percentage of Chihuahua puppies should the breeder expect to have long hair?

13. What is the predicted ratio of short-haired to long-haired offspring?

14. Which other crosses have a greater probability of producing Chihuahuas with the long-hair trait than the *Hh* x *Hh* cross? Circle all that apply.

A. *HH* x *Hh*

B. *hh* x *hh*

C. *Hh* x *hh*

D. None of these crosses

© Houghton Mifflin Harcourt

Artificial Selection Does Not Modify Genes

Advances in the scientific understanding of genes and inheritance improved selective breeding programs. For example, recessive traits are not always visible in an organism. Understanding inheritance patterns can help breeders make recessive traits more or less common in a population, even if the traits cannot be seen in the parents. Humans are still finding new ways to influence desired traits in living things. Biologists now understand how to change genes directly using molecular tools. The process of changing genes directly is called *genetic engineering*. However, artificial selection does not change genes. It only influences how common existing traits are in a population.

Language SmArts

Compare Mechanisms of Change in Species

15. Read the text for each photo to decide if humans or environmental factors are influencing traits. Identify each example as *natural selection*, *artificial selection*, or *genetic engineering*. Use evidence from the lesson to support your choices.

Example	Mechanism and evidence
Neon-colored tetras are produced when DNA from sea anemones, coral, or jellyfish is inserted into the genetic material of wild-type tetra fish.	
Dutch farmers carefully bred the pineberry, or "reverse strawberry," over several years. Cultivation begins with crossing a nearly extinct white strawberry plant with a red strawberry plant.	
Farmers want dairy cows to produce as much high-fat milk as possible. The DNA of beef and dairy cows have differences in genes that control milk production.	
This hummingbird's bill is long and curved. Its food source is nectar, which is found deep in flowers. Some flowers have long tube shapes.	

© Houghton Mifflin Harcourt • Image Credits: ©GloFish/Getty Images North America/Getty Images; ©jack_lisbon/iStock/Getty Images Plus/Getty Images; ©Wally Stemberger/Shutterstock; ©Ondrej Prosicky/Shutterstock

Applying Artificial Selection to Solve Problems

Artificial Selection as a Biotechnology

Artificial selection is a type of **biotechnology**—the use of biological understanding to solve practical problems. The root word, *technology*, implies that people use creativity to design and implement biological solutions. Using yeast to produce yogurt and cheese is biotechnology. Other examples are using bacteria to make antibiotics, to break down sewage, or to clean up oil spills. In each case, people use advances in the scientific understanding of a biological process to solve a problem or improve the quality of life.

16. Is natural selection considered a biotechnology? Why or why not?

Case Study: Artificial Selection of Corals

In 2005, the Caribbean lost 50% of its coral reefs due to a rise in the area's ocean temperatures. Warm water causes corals to get rid of the algae living in their tissues. This process is called *bleaching*. The bleached corals become weaker. Some corals may die from lack of food without the photosynthetic algae to provide nutrients.

Artificial selection might help corals become more tolerant of warm temperatures. Coral species from Australia have adapted to warmer waters. Breeding corals from Australia with ones found in colder regions introduces warmth-tolerance genes into more coral species. Scientists can continue selective breeding to increase the total number of corals with these genes.

These tanks are full of corals from different world regions. Selectively breeding coral types might help improve a coral species' ability to resist threats in its environment.

© Houghton Mifflin Harcourt • Image Credits: ©ANNE-CHRISTINE POUJOULAT/AFP/ Getty Images

Meeting Needs and Desires

When humans use artificial selection to protect coral, they are helping meet a variety of human needs and desires. Coral reefs are beautiful. This makes them a favorite spot for tourists to visit. Companies around reefs, such as ecotourism companies, hotels, restaurants, and local fisheries, provide many jobs. Coral reefs are also areas of high biodiversity. Therefore, there are many species and many individuals present. Ocean algae that live among reef systems provide a large percentage of the oxygen in Earth's air. Some medicines also come from coral reefs. For example, an enzyme used by corals to fight disease is an ingredient in medicines used to treat asthma and arthritis. Protecting reefs through artificial selection will also protect these valuable resources.

Healthy reef systems support nearly 4,000 species of fish. Scientists think there may be over a million undiscovered species that also live among the world's coral reefs.

17. What criteria must be met for artificial selection to be a successful solution to coral bleaching and the long-term success of coral reefs? Select all that apply.

A. Corals must have variation in their ability to survive changing temperatures.

B. The trait being influenced in corals must be beneficial to humans.

C. The offspring of corals must be able to reproduce in nature.

D. The ability to survive changing temperatures must involve heritable traits.

E. The artificial selection process must not harm healthy coral reefs.

EVIDENCE NOTEBOOK

18. What human needs or desires were met through the development of alpaca populations? Record your evidence.

© Houghton Mifflin Harcourt • Image Credits: ©Comstock/Stockbyte/Getty Images

Engineer It | Evaluate Uses of Artificial Selection Ocean water is also becoming more acidic. Higher acidity prevents corals from using carbonate to build their skeletons. An effective artificial selection solution will help corals hold on to algae. It will also increase the amount of carbonate corals uptake in increasingly warm and acidic ocean water. Two proposed solutions are given in the table.

Proposed solution	Description
Farming corals in several conditions	Corals are grown in different acidity levels and with different algae in order to find and breed the healthiest combination.
Exposing lab-raised corals to stress	Scientists think that the DNA of stressed corals changes in a way that makes them better able to withstand the same stress when it happens again. Corals that can best tolerate stress are chosen for breeding programs.

19. What do the proposed solutions for reducing coral bleaching have in common? Circle all that apply.

   A. They both include identifying variation in traits.

   B. They both include selectively breeding corals for desirable traits.

   C. They both include selectively breeding algae for desirable traits.

   D. They both depend on environmental factors to alter coral DNA.

20. Choose one of the solutions. Explain how it could be improved or expanded to help solve the problem of coral bleaching.

Analyze the Impacts of Artificial Selection on Society

Today's juicy corn is the result of thousands of years of selective breeding. Just five gene areas cause the differences between corn and teosinte, corn's ancestor. Farmers planted only seeds from plants with larger kernels or more cobs. Now, advances in genetics allow farmers to encourage pest and drought resistance in corn. Corn has become a *super crop*, grown in large amounts to meet many needs.

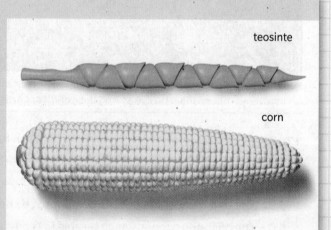

teosinte

corn

© Houghton Mifflin Harcourt

21. How have important crops that have been highly influenced by human breeding, such as corn, impacted society?

_____

_____

_____

_____

Continue Your Exploration

Name: _____   Date: _____

Check out the path below or go online to choose one of the other paths shown.

| Breeding Bacteria | • Hands-On Labs 👋
• Accidental Selection
• Propose Your Own Path | *Go online to choose one of these other paths.* |

Plants often depend on bacteria to help them get nutrients, fight disease, and resist environmental stress. Humans use plants in many ways, such as for food. Using artificial selection to encourage plant-helping traits in bacteria can help meet human needs. For example, scientists have learned that some bacteria help rice plants survive in areas with high temperatures and high soil acidity. Scientists are testing the use of these bacteria to help corals as oceans becomes warmer and more acidic! Using safe bacteria to promote plant health also reduces the need for fertilizers and pesticides that cause pollution.

Bacteria can help plants in many ways. Scientists use the steps below to identify and choose plant-helping bacteria.

STEP 1 Grow plants in soils treated with different types of plant-helping bacteria.

STEP 2 Compare the plants to find out which bacteria help them the most.

STEP 3 Collect bacteria from the healthiest plants for selective breeding.

STEP 4 Test the offspring bacteria in fresh soil with new plants.

STEP 5 Repeat Steps 1–4 to optimize the effects.

Once this process is complete, the selectively bred plant-helping bacteria can be sold to farmers to improve crop harvests.

These root nodules are the result of a plant-bacteria symbiosis. The bacteria help plants get nitrogen. The plants give the bacteria energy-rich sugars.

© Houghton Mifflin Harcourt • Image Credits: ©Dave Bevan/Alamy

153

1. How might the artificial selection of plant-helping bacteria affect society? Select all that apply.

   A. It boosts the economy by increasing farmer profits.

   B. It increases pollution due to pesticide use.

   C. It encourages partnerships between scientists and industry leaders.

   D. It reduces pollution from artificial fertilizers.

2. Is the process used to isolate and increase plant-helping bacteria an engineering solution? Use evidence from the passage to support your answer.

3. Scientists use genetic testing to identify specific genes present in organisms, including bacteria. How might this technology make it easier to breed plant-helping bacteria using artificial selection?

4. **Collaborate** Genetic engineering could also be used to increase plant-helping traits in bacteria. What advantages does the use of artificial selection provide compared to genetic engineering? Make a list of possible advantages to discuss with your class.

© Houghton Mifflin Harcourt

Can You Explain It?

Name: _____   Date: _____

How did humans cause alpacas to become different from vicuñas over time?

vicuña

alpaca

EVIDENCE NOTEBOOK

Refer to the notes in your Evidence Notebook to help you construct
an explanation for how humans influenced the development of alpaca
populations from vicuñas.

1. State your claim. Make sure your claim fully explains how humans influenced the
   development of alpaca populations.

2. Summarize the evidence you gathered to support your claim and explain
   your reasoning.

© Houghton Mifflin Harcourt • Image Credits: (l) ©Heeb Christian/Prisma Bildagentur AG/ Alamy; (r) ©Paul Springett C/Alamy

Checkpoints

Answer the following questions to check your understanding of the lesson.

Use the Punnett square to answer Questions 3 and 4.

3. What is the probability that these parents will produce a short-haired Chihuahua?

   A. 0%

   B. 25%

   C. 50%

   D. 100%

4. Which two individuals should be bred to produce the highest probability of having a long-haired Chihuahua?

   A. *HH* and *hh*

   B. *Hh* and *Hh*

   C. *Hh* and *hh*

   D. *HH* and *Hh*

Genotype: *HH*
Phenotype: short hair

Genotype: *hh*
Phenotype: long hair

	H	*H*
h	*Hh*	*Hh*
h	*Hh*	*Hh*

Use the photograph to answer Question 5.

5. What evidence in the photo suggests that roses have been influenced by artificial selection?

   A. The roses all have very soft petals.

   B. The roses display variety in only one trait.

   C. The roses display traits that appeal to humans.

   D. Some roses have more stripes or flecks than others.

---

6. How does artificial selection differ from natural selection? Circle all that apply.

   A. During artificial selection, the mating pairs are selected by humans, not the organisms.

   B. The outcomes of artificial selection are predictable.

   C. Artificial selection requires variety in a population.

   D. Artificial selection does not help a population adapt to its environment.

7. How are genetic engineering and artificial selection similar? Circle all that apply.

   A. They influence traits in organisms.

   B. They involve altering DNA sequences.

   C. They attempt to meet human needs or desires.

   D. They expand as scientific understanding of inheritance improves.

© Houghton Mifflin Harcourt • Image Credits: ©Jill Lang/Fotolia

Interactive Review

Complete this section to review the main concepts of the lesson.

People have used artificial selection for thousands of years to influence the inheritance of desired traits in living things.

A. What is required for artificial selection? Is an advanced understanding of genes needed?

Artificial selection influences the genotypes and phenotypes of populations.

B. How do Punnett squares help predict the outcomes of artificial selection?

Artificial selection helps meet the needs and desires of humans.

C. Explain an example of how artificial selection can help solve human problems.

© Houghton Mifflin Harcourt • Image Credits: (t) ©funwithfood/E+/Getty Images; (c) ©carlos Restrepo/Fotolia; (b) ©ANNE-CHRISTINE POUJOULAT/AFP/Getty Images

Genetic Engineering

This cat is producing proteins that cause it to glow green under certain types of light.

By the end of this lesson . . .

you will be able to explain how genetic engineering can be used to influence traits in organisms.

© Houghton Mifflin Harcourt • Image Credits: ©Mayo Clinic/Rex Features/AP Images

CAN YOU EXPLAIN IT?

How can goats produce spider silk proteins?

Spiders make silk, a type of protein that is light, strong, and flexible. Scientists have developed goats that produce spider silk proteins in their milk. The spider silk protein can be separated from the milk and then used by humans.

1. What are the advantages of getting spider silk from goats instead of spiders?

2. Do you think people could breed goats to produce spider silk proteins? Explain your answer.

 EVIDENCE NOTEBOOK As you explore the lesson, gather evidence to help explain what can cause goats to produce spider silk proteins.

© Houghton Mifflin Harcourt • Image Credits: (l) ©FLPA/Alamy; (r) ©John Anderson/Fotolia

Exploring Genetic Engineering Techniques

You may have friends with blue, green, or brown eyes. Eye color is an inherited *trait* that is passed from parents to offspring. Traits are controlled by genes. *Genes* are segments of DNA on chromosomes. Genes code for proteins that cause specific traits in an organism, such as eye color. Scientists can change genes to influence traits in organisms.

Inheritance of Eye Color

3. Eye color is a trait influenced by several genes. The *OCA2* and *HERC2* genes determine how much melanin pigment is produced in iris cells. More melanin leads to brown eyes. Less melanin leads to blue eyes. Complete the diagram using terms in the word bank.

WORD BANK
proteins
DNA
traits
genes

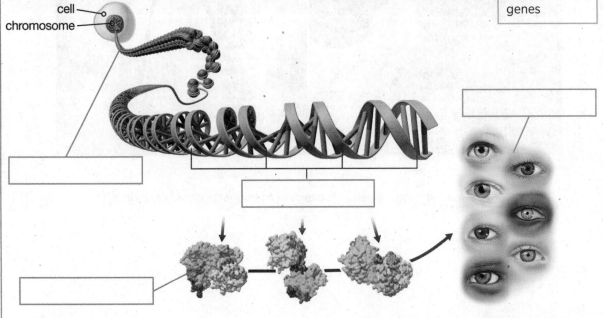

cell
chromosome

Genetic Engineering as Biotechnology

As scientists improve their understanding of the biological processes that connect genes to traits, they develop technologies to study and influence desired traits in organisms. **Genetic engineering** is the process of modifying DNA for practical purposes. Scientists might modify DNA for use in research, medicine, or agriculture. For example, soybean plants are important for oils and livestock feed. Soybeans are a genetically modified crop. Soybean crop health improved after scientists inserted genes for pest resistance into soybean seeds. Gene insertion is just one biotechnology used by genetic engineers. Other genetic engineering technologies encourage the production of specific proteins, or change genes to modify traits in organisms.

A caterpillar chewed holes in the leaves of this soybean plant. Inserting a pest resistance gene into soybeans can decrease damage due to pests.

© Houghton Mifflin Harcourt • Image Credits: ©SergioZacchi/iStock/Getty Images Plus/ Getty Images

Comparing Genetic Engineering and Artificial Selection

Humans have influenced the traits of organisms for thousands of years through artificial selection. *Artificial selection* is the process of breeding organisms to increase the frequency of desired traits in a population. Both artificial selection and genetic engineering influence the traits present in a population. For example, humans can improve pest resistance in soybeans by breeding plants that show increased resistance to pests *or* by inserting a pest-resistance gene. Influencing traits through genetic engineering can be more precise and faster than using artificial selection. In some cases, genetic engineering allows scientists to make changes to the traits of an organism that would not be possible through artificial selection.

Inserting a Gene into a Bacterium

Segments of DNA from one organism may be integrated into the DNA of a different organism. The simple structure of bacterial cells makes them good candidates for genetic engineering.

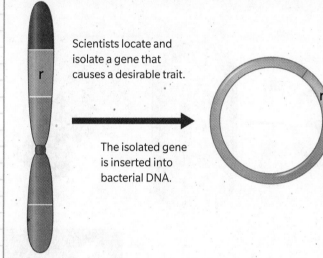

Scientists locate and isolate a gene that causes a desirable trait.

The isolated gene is inserted into bacterial DNA.

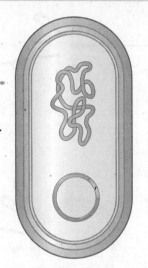

The bacterial DNA is inserted into a bacterium. The new trait is expressed when the bacterium uses the inserted gene to make proteins.

4. What is required to insert a new gene into a bacterium and for the bacterium to show the new trait? Select all that apply.

   A. proteins

   B. biotechnology

   C. cellular processes

   D. a breeding program

5. Discuss When inserting a new gene into an organism, the gene could come from the same species or it could come from a different species. Generate at least three questions you could research about each of these scenarios.

© Houghton Mifflin Harcourt

Milestones in Genetic Engineering

Rapid advancements in genetic engineering began in the early 1970s. Biologists saw that bacteria use special enzymes to repair their DNA. For example, bacteria use enzymes to cut and remove DNA that was inserted by a virus. *Viruses* are small particles that insert viral genetic information into host cells. The discovery about how bacteria use "cut and paste" enzymes inspired scientists to investigate how these enzymes could be used to solve human problems. Developments in genetic engineering reflect scientific progress. Scientists use creativity and existing technology to make new discoveries. This leads to increased understanding and chances for more exploration.

Recombination Technology

When a new gene is inserted into DNA, the DNA is called *recombinant DNA*. Recombinant DNA began by using *plasmids*, or small circles of bacterial DNA.

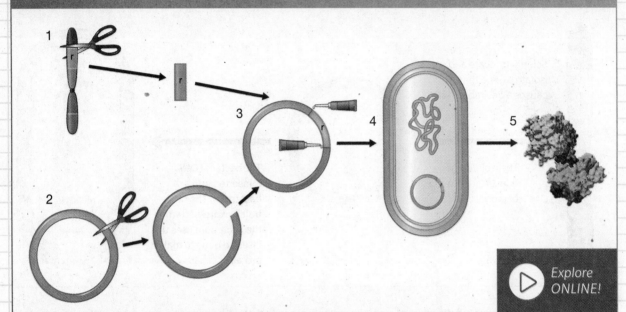

Explore ONLINE!

| **Step 1** The gene that controls a trait is located and cut from the chromosome. | **Step 2** The plasmid is opened using "cut" enzymes. | **Step 3** The new gene is added to the plasmid using "paste" enzymes. | **Step 4** The plasmid with the new gene is inserted into a bacterium. | **Step 5** The bacterium produces the new protein. |

6. Number the milestones of genetic engineering to show the progression of science.

_____ Foreign DNA is successfully inserted into the DNA of bacteria.

_____ Scientists confirm that the new genes give the bacteria new traits.

_____ "Cut and paste" enzymes are discovered by observing how bacteria use enzymes to destroy the DNA of invading viruses.

_____ Bacteria use inserted genes to make proteins, just as they do with their own genes.

© Houghton Mifflin Harcourt

Hands-On Lab
Model the Modification of Bacteria

You will model genetic modification of a bacterium using "cut and paste" enzymes. You will also analyze how genetic modification of bacteria can help humans.

Bacteria are unicellular organisms. Bacteria do not have nuclei. Instead, most of the genes are in a single, circular chromosome in the cytoplasm. The simple structure and rapid reproduction of bacteria make them a good choice for scientific research.

MATERIALS

- colored beads (to fit on pipe cleaner)
- colored pencils
- pipe cleaners
- scissors

Procedure

STEP 1 Locate the circular chromosome and the plasmids in the diagram. Use evidence from the diagram to make a list of traits controlled by the bacterium's DNA.

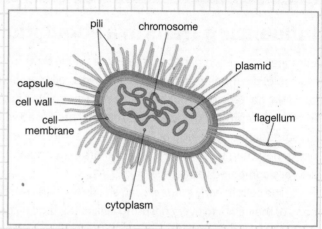

This bacterium has a single large chromosome and several smaller circles of DNA called plasmids. The plasmids contain few genes. They are not essential for the bacterium's survival.

STEP 2 Build a pipe cleaner plasmid to model a circular plasmid in the bacterium. To model DNA bases, use beads similar in color to the letters in the sequence given. Add the correct sequence of DNA "bases" to the pipe cleaner and then twist the free ends together.

DNA sequence: TTGAGCGCATTGCGT

STEP 3 The "cut" enzyme cuts the plasmid between an ATT sequence and a GCG sequence. Cut your plasmid in the correct location. The scissors model the enzyme in this step.

STEP 4 Choose one of the genes from the table to insert into your plasmid. Add the correct sequences of bases. Then "paste" (twist) the free ends together.

Function of protein encoded by gene	DNA sequence of gene
stops the bacterium from building pili that help the bacterium infect cells	TTGAA
causes bacterium to burst	GCGTA
increases production of a protein used in livestock feed	ATTTA

© Houghton Mifflin Harcourt

Analysis

STEP 5 Draw the modified bacterium with its new trait.

STEP 6 How might a population of bacteria with this new trait be helpful for people?

Influencing Traits in a Population

Engineers can insert genes that cause desirable traits in an organism. In order to be heritable, the modification must be made to cells passed to offspring. This is easy in bacteria. Bacteria divide in half and pass a complete copy of their DNA to their offspring. In sexually reproducing organisms, genetic modification will only be heritable if it occurs in reproductive cells—egg or sperm—or in early embryos. This makes it more difficult to use genetic engineering to influence traits in a population of organisms that reproduce sexually compared to bacteria.

The cells in early embryos can still develop into any cell type. They pass an identical copy of their DNA to every offspring cell, including any genetic modifications. During the process of *cell differentiation*, cells become specialized for a specific function. Once cells differentiate into various types, such as muscle cells or blood cells, genetic modifications made to the cells will only pass to the offspring cells of that cell type.

Cell Differentiation in Embryos

Early embryo cells differentiate into the different cell types found in an organism. This diagram shows three examples of specialized cell types.

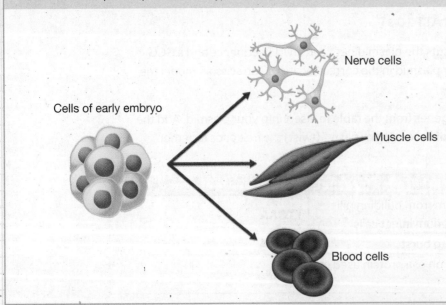

Cells of early embryo

Nerve cells

Muscle cells

Blood cells

© Houghton Mifflin Harcourt

7. Do the Math If all of a poisonous frog's eggs are genetically engineered right after fertilization to include a gene that prevents poison production, what is the ratio of poisonous to non-poisonous frogs in the offspring?

A. 1:0

B. 1:2

C. 0:1

D. 1:1

EVIDENCE NOTEBOOK

8. How could genetic engineering cause goats to produce a new protein? Record your evidence.

Genetic Modification of Bacteria

Genetic engineering can be used to help solve human problems. People with diabetes need a dependable supply of insulin. Insulin is a protein that helps regulate blood sugar. Scientists have modified bacteria to produce insulin for human use. Large numbers of the modified bacteria can be farmed to produce large amounts of insulin.

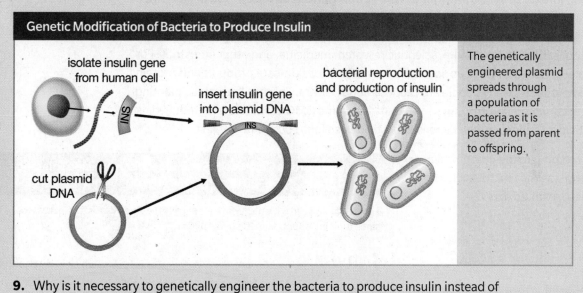

Genetic Modification of Bacteria to Produce Insulin

isolate insulin gene from human cell

cut plasmid DNA

insert insulin gene into plasmid DNA

bacterial reproduction and production of insulin

The genetically engineered plasmid spreads through a population of bacteria as it is passed from parent to offspring.

9. Why is it necessary to genetically engineer the bacteria to produce insulin instead of inserting the insulin gene in humans?

_____

_____

_____

_____

_____

_____

_____

_____

_____

© Houghton Mifflin Harcourt

Evaluating Genetic Modification

Genetically engineered crops, especially those not intended for the human food supply, are common in the United States and other industrialized nations. For example, genetically modified soybean plants now make up more than 80% of all soybean crops around the world. Many of these soybeans are used for animal feed. The use of genetically modified crops is increasing. Some modified crops are hardier and more productive than non-modified crops.

These cotton plants contain genes to resist the herbicides that farmers use to kill weeds.

10. Why might farmers want to grow cotton plants that are resistant to herbicides?

Genetically Modified Organisms

Inserting foreign DNA into an organism results in a **genetically modified organism,** or GMO. These organisms are often called *transgenic* because genetic modification allows genes to cross the normal barriers between species (*trans* means "across"). GMOs have applications in agriculture, scientific research, medicine, and other industries. For example, genetically modified soybeans provide oils for skin-care products and protein for food products. Many people are cautious about GMOs. This has limited the planting of genetically modified crops in some countries. Some GMO crops allow for reduced use of pesticides. Others require increased pesticide use for a successful harvest.

11. According to the graph, which crop was the first to reach 75% GMO-planted acres?

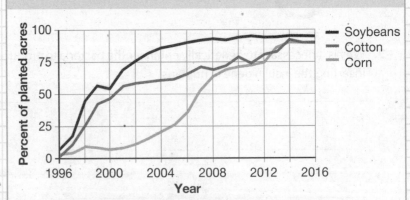

Adoption of Crops Genetically Engineered for Herbicide Tolerance (United States, 1996–2016)

The number of acres planted with genetically modified crops has increased since their introduction in the mid-1990s.

Sources: USDA, Economic Research Service using data from Fernandez-Comejo and McBride (2002) for the years 1996–99 and USDA, National Agricultural Statistics Service, June Agricultural Survey for the years 2000–16.

12. There may be more support for the genetic modification of a crop if the crop is not used for human food. What pattern in the graph might be explained by this statement?

A. the different adoption rates between cotton and soybeans

B. the different adoption rates between cotton and corn

C. the current adoption level of soybeans, cotton, and corn

© Houghton Mifflin Harcourt • Image Credits: ©STEVEN SIEWERT/Fairfax Media/Getty Images

Case Study: Glowing Mosquitoes

Malaria and dengue fever are human diseases that are spread by mosquitoes. Scientists can insert a gene that causes mosquitoes to die if they do not receive a specific chemical. Scientists insert a fluorescent gene from jellyfish at the same time to track which mosquitoes have been successfully modified. Researchers release only modified male mosquitoes to the wild because male mosquitoes do not bite humans. When female mosquitoes in the wild mate with the modified males, the offspring inherit the modified gene and die without access to the chemical. This reduces mosquito populations and can slow the spread of some human diseases. However, the release of genetically modified mosquitoes into the wild raises concerns about the impact on birds and bats that may eat the GMOs.

These mosquito larvae glow. Their cells have genes from jellyfish that make fluorescent proteins.

The Impact of Genetically Modified Mosquitoes	
Effect on individuals	Human individuals experience reduced exposure to diseases carried by mosquitoes, including malaria and dengue fever.
Effect on society	Society benefits from reduced health care costs associated with malaria and dengue fever. The money saved can be used for other beneficial projects in communities.
Effect on the environment	The release of genetically modified mosquitoes might have negative impacts on birds or bats that feed on mosquitoes.

Case Study: Research Mice

Some research mice are genetically modified for scientific research. *Knockout mice* have a gene in their DNA "knocked out" or disrupted. Scientists then observe the mice to see how their traits change. This helps scientists identify the gene's function. Humans and mice have similar DNA, so research with knockout mice can help scientists learn what human genes do. For example, knockout mice research has provided data about genes involved in cancer and anxiety in humans. However, knockout mice are not a perfect research tool. Knocking out an important gene can cause developmental problems in the mice. Also, data from knockout mice studies cannot always be applied to humans.

A gene has been "knocked out" in the mouse on the left. Scientists use knockout mice to learn what genes do.

13. Identify whether the impacts described in the table relate to individuals, society, or the environment.

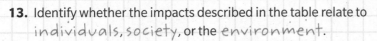

The Impact of Genetically Modified Mice	
	Knockout mice stay in a lab to limit the chance of spreading modified genes to wild mice.
	Researchers use information from knockout mice to treat similar diseases in humans.
	Knockout mice might be hurt by changes made through genetic engineering.

© Houghton Mifflin Harcourt • Image Credits: (t) ©Sinclair Stammers/Science Source; (b) ©Science Source

Case Study: Pharmaceutical Chickens

In 2015, officials in the United States approved the farming of genetically engineered chickens. The chickens produce a special protein in their eggs that can be used to treat a human disorder. The protein is isolated from the eggs and given to people who lack the protein in their bodies. Without this protein, humans cannot break down fat molecules. The condition is fatal to infants and causes heart disease in adults. There is no other effective treatment for the disorder.

Plants, bacteria, and other organisms have been genetically modified for medical purposes. Goats can be modified to produce a chemical in their milk that breaks down blood clots in humans. Using mammals to produce pharmaceutical chemicals in their milk can be effective. Milk production is a natural process, and milking does not harm the animals.

Chickens can be genetically modified to produce a pharmaceutical protein in their eggs.

The Impact of Genetically Modified Chickens	
Effect on individuals	Humans with a protein disorder will experience fewer deaths and reduced illness by receiving replacement protein from the chicken eggs. Laying eggs is a natural process, so the chickens are not harmed.
Effect on society	Some medical chemicals need cellular processes for production. Using GMOs to produce these chemicals provides medicines that cannot be made in a laboratory.
Effect on the environment	The introduction of GMOs into communities can be risky. Scientists try to prevent the transfer of genetically modified DNA by isolating GMOs. Some people worry that modified genes will accidentally spread to wild species.

14. Which of the following are positive impacts that genetically modified chickens have on society? Circle all that apply.

    A. production of pharmaceuticals that cannot be manufactured

    B. improved medical care for humans

    C. increasing numbers of GMOs in communities

    D. production of proteins that cure all diseases

15. **Discuss** The use of animals in scientific research can help society but the rights of animals must be considered. How can you apply the concept of ethics to the subject of animal testing?

© Houghton Mifflin Harcourt • Image Credits: ©Ornitolog82/Fotolia

16. What evidence suggests that genetic modification is involved in goats that produce spider silk in their milk? Record your evidence.

Engineer It

Evaluate Impacts of Genetically Modified Crops

Bacillus thuringiensis (Bt) is a bacterium that makes proteins that kill pests. Scientists isolated the Bt gene and inserted it into the DNA of corn seeds. The result is Bt corn. Bt corn is a GMO that is resistant to leaf-eating caterpillars.

Corn can be genetically modified to protect the plants from caterpillar damage.

17. Complete the table to explain how genetically modified corn might impact individuals, society, and the environment.

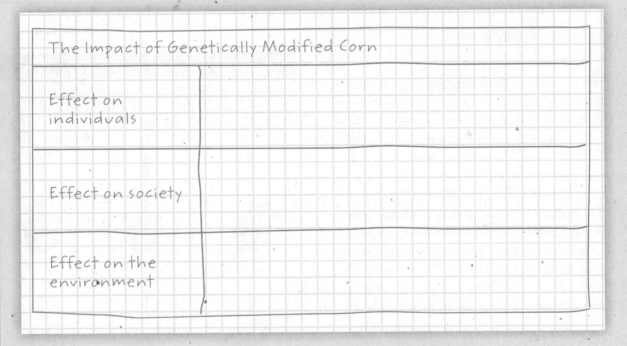

The Impact of Genetically Modified Corn	
Effect on individuals	
Effect on society	
Effect on the environment	

18. Would you grow genetically modified corn if you were a farmer? Provide your reasoning.

_____

_____

_____

_____

_____

© Houghton Mifflin Harcourt • Image Credits: ©sanddebeautheill/iStock/Getty Images Plus/ Getty Images

Evaluating Gene Therapy

Genetic engineering is not limited to genetic modification using bacteria. Other microbes and molecules can also be used to insert or influence genes in similar ways. For example, viruses are used in genetic engineering. Viruses inject viral genes into a cell. The cell then produces viral proteins that are assembled into new viruses. Scientists can change viruses so that they inject desirable genes into cells instead of viral genes.

19. Discuss What might be some advantages and disadvantages of using viruses in genetic engineering to treat human diseases?

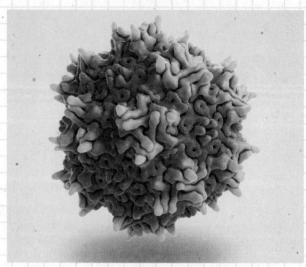

Scientists often choose *adenoviruses* to deliver genes to target cells. These viruses inject their genetic material into a cell's nucleus.

Gene Therapy

Advances in biotechnology allow scientists to treat certain diseases. **Gene therapy** is a technique that uses genes to treat or prevent disease. Gene therapy may be used to insert helpful genes or to remove harmful genes. It may also be used to insert "suicide genes" that cause cell death. This is a promising treatment for cancer.

Most gene therapies are still being tested and studied. To be successfully treated with gene therapy, a disease must have a genetic cause and scientists must know which genes cause the disease. Also, the disease should involve one or only a few genes. Finally, the affected genes must be accessible for treatment for gene therapy to be successful.

One gene therapy success story involves children born with immune cells that do not work. A single gene normally active in bone marrow causes the disease. Therapy involves taking bone marrow cells from a patient, inserting the correct gene, and replacing diseased bone marrow cells with modified cells. Without treatment, children born with the disorder must live in germ-free plastic bubbles. Gene therapy allows these children to live healthy lives.

Types of Gene Therapy

Gene therapy can involve adding a functional gene, blocking a malfunctioning gene, or causing a malfunctioning cell to die.

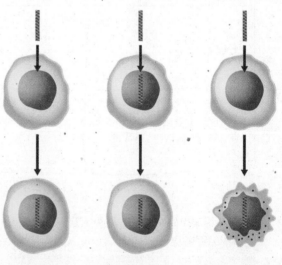

Addition of a therapeutic gene provides normal cell function.

Addition of a therapeutic gene blocks a malfunctioning gene, providing normal cell function.

Addition of a harmful gene produces a lethal substance and the targeted cell dies.

© Houghton Mifflin Harcourt • Image Credits: ©Science Picture Co./Alamy

Methods of Gene Delivery

Gene therapy may involve direct or indirect delivery of therapeutic genes. In *direct gene delivery*, a therapeutic gene is inserted into a virus. Then the genetically modified virus is delivered directly to the target site. In *indirect gene delivery*, a therapeutic gene is inserted into a virus. Cells are extracted from the patient. The genetically modified virus is used to introduce the gene to the cells outside of the body. The genetically modified cells are delivered to the target site.

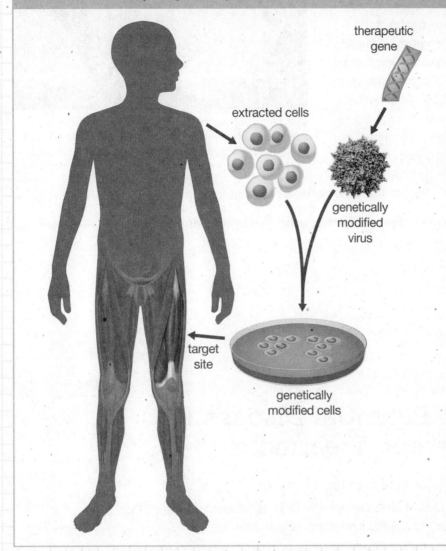

therapeutic gene

extracted cells

genetically modified virus

target site

genetically modified cells

Indirect Gene Delivery

1. **Identify Target Cells** Cells receiving therapeutic genes must be in an isolated area.

2. **Prepare Gene for Delivery** A therapeutic gene is inserted into a virus or other delivery mechanism.

3. **Remove Cells for Modification** Diseased cells are removed from a patient so they can be modified in a lab.

4. **Inject Virus into Extracted Cells** The virus carrying the therapeutic gene is injected into cells removed from the patient's body. Modified cells are grown in the lab.

5. **Deliver Modified Cells** Modified cells are delivered to the patient through injection at a target site.

20. Why might scientists choose indirect delivery instead of direct delivery for a gene therapy?

A. Indirect delivery methods take less time than direct delivery methods.

B. Direct gene delivery is only possible if the target area is accessible.

C. Genetically modified cells are easier to deliver to the target area than genetically modified viruses.

D. Indirect delivery allows scientists to make sure the cells have been correctly modified and are producing the protein.

21. Why are diseases involving many different genes poor candidates for gene therapy?

© Houghton Mifflin Harcourt

Impacts of Gene Therapy

Gene therapy has the potential to treat many diseases. The field of gene therapy is still new. Advances in biotechnology are improving gene delivery methods. While the future of gene therapy looks promising, it faces many challenges. Gene therapy raises many ethical concerns about whether human DNA should be changed. Genetic engineering is also costly. Gene therapy may not be available to poorer populations. Gene therapy can disrupt the function of healthy genes in target cells, and long-term effects are uncertain. New genes often result from natural mutations. Over time, evolutionary forces will minimize genes and traits with negative effects. New genes resulting from genetic engineering do not go through the same evolutionary process.

Cystic fibrosis is a genetic disease that causes persistent lung infections. Treatment includes inhaling medicine through a nebulizer. Gene therapies are being tested for this disease.

22. What are the requirements a disease must meet for gene therapy to be an effective option for treatment? Circle all that apply.

   A. It must have a genetic cause.

   B. It should involve many genes.

   C. Target cells must be accessible.

   D. Target cells must be found throughout the patient's body.

Language SmArts

Identify a Potential Disease for Gene Therapy Treatment

Consider what scientists know about these three diseases:

- The predisposition to have **heart disease** is inherited. The disease is influenced by other factors, including age, diet, high blood pressure, and smoking.

- A single gene causes **hemophilia.** Hemophilia results in a lack of clotting proteins in the blood. Clotting proteins are produced in the liver. The lack of clotting proteins can lead to severe bleeding and joint damage.

- People with **type I diabetes** produce little or no insulin. Insulin is needed to move sugar from the blood into cells. Type I diabetes involves multiple genes. It is triggered by environmental factors.

23. Which disease has the best potential for treatment with gene therapy? Defend your answer using evidence from the text and explain what criteria you used.

   _____

   _____

   _____

   _____

© Houghton Mifflin Harcourt • Image Credits: ©Idaho Statesman/Chris Butler/AP Images

Continue Your Exploration

Name: _____   Date: _____

Check out the path below or go online to choose one of the other paths shown.

| Careers in Science | • Hands-On Labs ✋
• Applications of Cloning
• Propose Your Own Path | Go online to choose one of these other paths. |

Bioethicist

Ethics are a set of ideas about what is right and wrong that help govern the actions of individuals and societies. Science often involves ethics. Bioethicists study the influence of societal values on science, such as religious concerns or relevant laws. Since cultures vary, what seems ethical in one place may not be considered ethical in another. Bioethicists conduct research and help people make decisions. They weigh the pros and cons of different science methods against important human values.

Since genetic engineering directly affects living organisms, it raises many ethical questions. For example, scientists have inserted genes from other species into rice to address vitamin A deficiency in certain human populations. The unique yellow rice is promising for human health. However, many people are concerned that the modified crops could trigger allergies, cause new disease, or spread genes to other species through cross-pollination or by being eaten by animals. This is an ethical issue because the needs of humans and the needs of the environment are in conflict. Bioethicists can help people work together to identify solutions that minimize these types of conflicts.

Beta-carotene is a plant pigment that gives carrots their color. This "golden rice" has been genetically modified to produce beta-carotene, a source of vitamin A.

People disagree about the benefits and safety of GMOs. Bioethicists can help people on both sides of the issue understand how values influence scientific methods and decisions.

© Houghton Mifflin Harcourt • Image Credits: (l) ©LOUIE DOUVIS/Fairfax Media/Getty Images; (r) ©RAJESH JANTILAL/AFP/Getty Images

Continue Your Exploration

1. In what ways does genetic engineering involve ethics? Circle all that apply.

    A. Altering genes affects humans and other living beings.

    B. Changing genes can have unexpected consequences.

    C. The decisions scientists make when using genetic engineering are based only on facts.

    D. Using technology to meet human needs can conflict with meeting the needs of other species or the environment.

2. Explain the ethical conflict that might arise from the genetic engineering of rice.

3. What are the differences between the questions scientists and bioethicists try to answer?

© Houghton Mifflin Harcourt

4. **Collaborate** Some children cannot produce enough growth hormone (GH) for normal bone development. Work with a group to create a poster that shows the criteria and constraints that might guide genetic engineers as they design solutions for producing GH for humans using other animals, such as pigs or cows. Which criteria and constraints involve ethics?

Can You Explain It?

Name: _____   Date: _____

How can goats produce spider silk proteins?

© Houghton Mifflin Harcourt • Image Credits: (l) ©FLPA/Alamy; (r) ©John Anderson/Fotolia

EVIDENCE NOTEBOOK

Refer to the notes in your Evidence Notebook to help you construct an explanation for what can cause goats to produce spider silk proteins.

1. State your claim. Make sure your claim fully explains genetic changes that allow goats to produce spider silk proteins.

2. Summarize the evidence you have gathered to support your claim and explain your reasoning.

Checkpoints

Answer the following questions to check your understanding of the lesson.

Use the photo of weeds in a cotton field to answer Question 3.

3. This field was sprayed with an herbicide and specific plants survived. What might cause herbicide resistance in the cotton plants or weeds in this field? Select all that apply.

   A. Scientists modified the cotton DNA to resist the herbicide.

   B. Some weeds naturally resist herbicide better than others.

   C. Cotton became herbicide resistant over thousands of years.

   D. Bees transferred herbicide resistance from cotton to weeds.

4. Why are viruses used to deliver therapeutic genes to target cells? Circle all that apply.

   A. scientists can modify viral DNA

   B. viruses carry many beneficial genes

   C. viruses can direct cells to make specific proteins

   D. viruses can be injected directly into cells

5. Some cause-and-effect relationships can only be explained using probability, such as the likelihood that an offspring will inherit a particular trait from one of its parents. Artificial selection increases / decreases the likelihood that offspring will inherit a desirable trait. Genetic engineering can / cannot bring the likelihood of inheritance of a desirable trait to 100%.

6. What is an advantage of using genetically modified mammals to produce desirable proteins in their milk?

   A. It is easy to genetically modify mammals.

   B. It is difficult to isolate the desirable proteins.

   C. Milk production is a natural process, so there are few negative impacts to the mammals.

   D. Genetic modification of mammals raises few ethical concerns.

Use the eye diagram to answer Question 7.

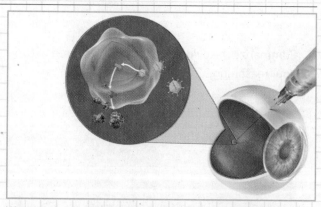

7. Why is wet macular degeneration a good candidate for gene therapy? Circle all that apply.

   A. The gene therapy is delivered by injection.

   B. The gene therapy makes a single protein that blocks new blood vessels causing the eye disease.

   C. The target cells in the eye are easily accessible.

   D. The modified cell produces new proteins.

Wet macular degeneration is an eye disease caused by leaking blood vessels. A gene therapy has been made that produces a protein that blocks the production of new blood vessels.

© Houghton Mifflin Harcourt • Image Credits: ©Betsy Blaney/AP Images

Interactive Review

Complete this section to review the main concepts of the lesson.

Genetic engineering involves the modification of genes for practical purposes.

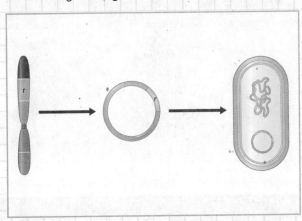

A. Describe the process genetic engineers use to insert genes into a bacterium's DNA so that it produces new proteins.

Inserting a new gene into an organism results in a genetically modified organism (GMO). The introduction of GMOs impacts individuals, society, and the environment.

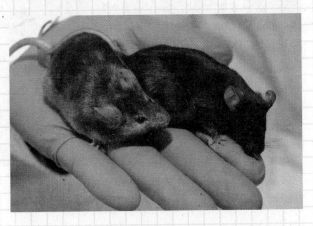

B. What are some impacts of genetically modified organisms on society?

Gene therapy is an experimental technique that uses genes to treat or prevent disease.

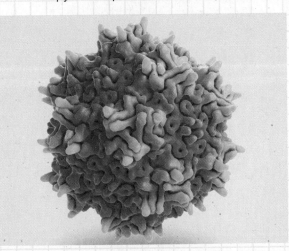

C. Explain the different delivery techniques used to deliver therapeutic genes to target cells.

© Houghton Mifflin Harcourt • Image Credits: (c) ©Science Source; (b) ©Science Picture Co./Alamy

Choose one of the activities to explore how this unit connects to other topics.

☐ Environmental Science Connection

Pollution-Fighting Trees At the University of Washington, scientists have genetically engineered poplar trees to take up as much as 91% of a common groundwater pollutant, called *trichlorethylene*. The engineered trees break this chemical down into harmless byproducts. Regular poplar trees only remove about 3% of this contaminant.

Research other ways poplar trees have been genetically modified. Explain the effects these modified trees might have on the environment and society. Make a pamphlet that combines text and images. Provide at least three credible sources.

☐ Social Studies Connection

Artificial Selection and Chinese Culture Goldfish were first domesticated in China over 1,000 years ago during the Tang dynasty. People began to breed the gold variety as a sign of wealth. Over the years, more varieties of goldfish have been bred, such as the bubble-eyed goldfish, first bred in 1908. This fish has enlarged fluid-filled sacs beneath its eyes.

Research another example of an animal or plant that has been influenced genetically over time by Chinese culture. Explain the connection between culture and the desired traits. Present your findings in a multimedia presentation.

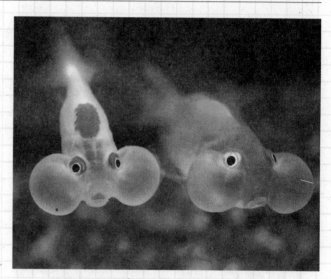

☐ Art Connection

Bioart When artists work with materials such as living tissue, bacteria, or other living organisms, the practice is called *bioart*. Sometimes the art pieces have a genetic engineering component to them. In one example of bioart, the artist hybridized a pink petunia and his own genes.

Research bioart and choose an artist or a specific art piece that uses genetic engineering. Research the method the artist used to create the art piece. Make a presentation that includes images, an explanation of how the artist achieved the artwork, and a summary of any ethical issues that might be related to the artwork.

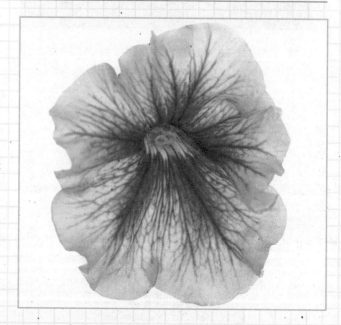

© Houghton Mifflin Harcourt • Image Credits: (t) ©Vladimir Mulder/Shutterstock; (c) ©Toru Kobayashi/EyeEm/Getty Images; (b) ©Irabel8/Shutterstock

Name: _____   Date: _____

Complete this review to check your understanding of the unit.

Use the image to answer Questions 1–3.

1. These flowers are delphinium hybrids. They are the result of selective pressures through artificial selection in nature / by humans.

2. Which traits were likely selected for in these plants? Select all that apply.

   A. flower color

   B. plant height

   C. traits that are genetically based

   D. traits that are not genetically based

3. What are some ways this species of flower might have evolved naturally? Select all that apply.

   A. Plant height might be selected based on ability to access enough sunlight.

   B. Flower color might be selected based on the preference of pollinators in the area.

   C. Plant shape might be selected based on the availability of space in the area.

   D. Petal shape might be selected based on the shape humans most prefer.

Use the chart to answer Question 4.

Disease	Description	Cause
Sickle cell disease	A hereditary form of anemia in which red blood cells are sickle-shaped, resulting in low oxygen levels in the blood.	Mutations in the hemoglobin-beta gene found on chromosome 11
Tay-Sachs disease	A rare, inherited disorder that destroys nerve cells in the brain and spinal cord.	Mutations in the HEXA gene
Heart disease (atherosclerosis)	A buildup of plaque causes arteries to narrow and makes it harder for blood to flow.	Multiple genetic and environmental contributions
Diabetes	The body's ability to produce or respond to insulin is impaired, causing high glucose levels in the blood and urine.	Multiple genetic and environmental contributions

4. Sickle cell disease / Diabetes would be more promising for gene therapy because it is caused by one gene / multiple genes.

5. Which of the following are methods of gene therapy? Select all that apply.

   A. adding a malfunctioning gene

   B. adding a functional gene

   C. blocking a malfunctioning gene

   D. causing a malfunctioning cell to die

© Houghton Mifflin Harcourt

6. Think about how each process in the table relates to inheritance. Then complete the table by describing the human influence, outcomes, risks, and benefits of each process.

Process	Human influence	Outcome	Risks	Benefits
Artificial selection	Humans control the reproduction of plants or animals.			
Genetic modification				
Gene therapy				

© Houghton Mifflin Harcourt

Name: _____

Date: _____

Use the photos to answer Questions 7–10.

This corn has been influenced by artificial selection and genetic modification.

This wheat has been influenced only by artificial selection.

7. Describe the types of traits that can be influenced in these food crops.

8. How are these examples of human influence on traits similar?

9. How are these examples of human influence on traits different?

10. Which is associated with a greater risk for negative impacts on the environment? Use evidence and reasoning to justify your answer.

© Houghton Mifflin Harcourt • Image Credits: (l) ©meandar/Shutterstock; (r) ©Teemu Tretjakov/EyeEm/Getty Images

Use the diagram to answer Questions 11–14.

Blood Clotting Protein Production

Some people have disorders that prevent blood from clotting properly. Scientists have identified a gene related to normal blood clotting in humans.

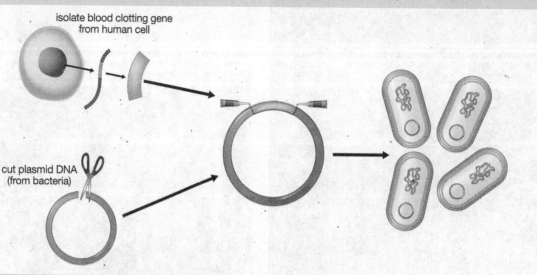

isolate blood clotting gene
from human cell

cut plasmid DNA
(from bacteria)

11. Describe what is happening in this process.

12. Why are bacteria used in this process?

13. What is the connection between the gene, protein, and trait in this example?

14. What is the final product of this process and how might it be used?

© Houghton Mifflin Harcourt

Name: _____   Date: _____

Should we light our street with bioluminescent trees?

Imagine that you have read about research that is being done to try to produce glowing trees. These trees would be genetically modified to be *bioluminescent*—they could produce light without electricity. You are on the city council, and you think it would be worth investing in this research. One day, perhaps these glowing trees could light the streets and park sidewalks in your city! Your task is to create a presentation to inform the rest of the city council, so the council can make an informed decision about investing in this research.

Genes from this bioluminescent mushroom could potentially be used to genetically modify trees.

The steps below will help guide your research and develop your recommendation.

1. **Conduct Research** Describe how you will evaluate your sources for credibility, accuracy, and bias. Why is it important for a source to support claims with evidence?

2. **Conduct Research** What is bioluminescence? What organisms in nature are bioluminescent?

© Houghton Mifflin Harcourt • Image Credits: (l) ©Nature Picture library/Alamy; (r) ©Jedrzej Kaminski/EyeEm/Getty Images

3. **Conduct Research** What other types of organisms have been genetically modified to glow? Choose one of these organisms and determine what need or problem this genetic modification helped to solve.

4. **Evaluate Data** Based on what you have learned about genetic modification and modifying organisms to glow, evaluate the benefits and potential risks of bioluminescent trees.

5. **Generate Questions** Create a list of questions that you would want the scientists who are researching bioluminescent trees to answer.

6. **Make a Recommendation** Explain whether or not you think the city council should invest in the research on bioluminescent trees. Might your recommendation change based on the answers you receive from the research scientists?

7. **Communicate** Create a presentation for the city council that summarizes your findings.

✓ **Self-Check**

	I researched bioluminescence and other organisms that have been genetically modified to glow.	
	I evaluated the risks and benefits of genetically modifying an organism.	
	I generated questions about the potential impacts of bioluminscent trees and made a recommendation for the city council.	
	I created a presentation that clearly communicates my findings.	

© Houghton Mifflin Harcourt

Glossary

			Pronunciation Key				
Sound	Symbol	Example	Respelling	Sound	Symbol	Example	Respelling
ă	a	pat	PAT	ŏ	ah	bottle	BAHT'l
ā	ay	pay	PAY	ō	oh	toe	TOH
âr	air	care	KAIR	ô	aw	caught	KAWT
ä	ah	father	FAH•ther	ôr	ohr	roar	ROHR
är	ar	argue	AR•gyoo	oi	oy	noisy	NOYZ•ee
ch	ch	chase	CHAYS	o͞o	u	book	BUK
ĕ	e	pet	PET	o͞o	oo	boot	BOOT
ĕ (at end of a syllable)	eh	settee lessee	seh•TEE leh•SEE	ou	ow	pound	POWND
ĕr	ehr	merry	MEHR•ee	s	s	center	SEN•ter
ē	ee	beach	BEECH	sh	sh	cache	CASH
g	g	gas	GAS	ŭ	uh	flood	FLUHD
ĭ	i	pit	PIT	ûr	er	bird	BERD
ĭ (at end of a syllable)	ih	guitar	gih•TAR	z	z	xylophone	ZY•luh•fohn
ī	y eye (only for a complete syllable)	pie island	PY EYE•luhnd	z	z	bags	BAGZ
îr	ir	hear	HIR	zh	zh	decision	dih•SIZH •uhn
j	j	germ	JERM	ə	uh	around broken focus	uh•ROWND BROH•kuhn FOH•kuhs
k	k	kick	KIK	ər	er	winner	WIN•er
ng	ng	thing	THING	th	th	thin they	THIN THAY
ngk	ngk	bank	BANGK	w	w	one	WUHN
				wh	hw	whether	HWETH•er

© Houghton Mifflin Harcourt

adaptation (ad•ap•TAY•shuhn)
an inherited trait that improves an individual's ability to survive and reproduce in a particular environment (87)
adaptación un carácter heredado que mejora la capacidad de un individuo para sobrevivir y reproducirse en un determinado ambiente

allele frequency (uh•LEEL•FREE•kwuhn•see)
the proportion of gene copies in a population that are a given allele, expressed as a percentage (97)
frecuencia alélica la proporción de copias de un gene presentes en una población que son un alelo determinado, expresada como un porcentaje

anatomy (uh•NAT•uh•mee)
the bodily structure of an organism (51)
anatomía la estructura corporal de un organismo

artificial selection (ar•tuh•FISH•uhl sih•LEK•shuhn)
the human practice of breeding animals or plants that have certain desired traits (145)
selección artificial la práctica humana de criar animales o cultivar plantas que tienen ciertos caracteres deseados

biotechnology (by•oh•tek•NAHL•uh•jee)
the use and application of living things and biological processes (150)
biotecnología el uso y la aplicación de seres vivos y procesos biológicos

common ancestry (KAHM•uhn AN•ses•tree)
the idea that organisms share a common ancestor at some point in the past; that all living organisms and all fossil organisms can be traced back to one or a few ancestor organisms or cells (48)
ascendencia común la idea de que los organismos tuvieron un ancestro en común en algún momento del pasado; de que el origen de todos los organismos vivos y todos los organismos fósiles se remonta a uno o algunos organismos o células ancestrales

DNA (dee•en•AY)
deoxyribonucleic acid, a molecule that is present in all living cells and that contains the information that determines the traits that a living thing inherits and needs to live (78)
AND ácido desoxirribonucleico, una molécula que está presente en todas las células vivas y que contiene la información que determina los caracteres que un ser vivo hereda y necesita para vivir

embryology (em•bree•AHL•uh•jee)
the study of the development of an animal from the fertilized egg to the newly born or hatched organism (53)
embriología estudio de cómo un animal se desarrolla a partir del óvulo fertilizado hasta convertirse en un organismo recién nacido

evolution (ev•uh•LOO•shuhn)
the process in which inherited characteristics within a population change over generations such that new species sometimes arise (48, 96)
evolución el proceso por medio del cual las características heredadas dentro de una población cambian con el transcurso de las generaciones de manera tal que a veces surgen nuevas especies

extinction (ek•STINGK•shuhn)
the death of every member of a species (17, 34, 121)
extinción la muerte de todos los miembros de una especie

fossil (FAHS•uhl)
the trace or remains of an organism that lived long ago, most commonly preserved in sedimentary rock (6)
fósil los indicios o los restos de un organismo que vivió hace mucho tiempo, comúnmente preservados en las rocas sedimentarias

fossil record (FAHS•uhl REK•erd)
the history of life in the geologic past as indicated by the traces or remains of living things (17)
registro fósil la historia de la vida en el pasado geológico según la indican los rastros o restos de seres vivos

gene (JEEN)
one set of instructions for an inherited trait (79)
gene un conjunto de instrucciones para un carácter heredado

gene therapy (JEEN THER•uh•pee)
a technique that places a gene into a cell to correct a hereditary disease or to improve the genome (170)
terapia genética una técnica que coloca un gene en una célula para corregir una enfermedad hereditaria o para mejorar el genoma

genetically modified organism (juh•NET•ik•lee MAHD•uh•fyd OHR•guh•niz•uhm)
an organism containing genetic material that has been artificially altered to produce a desired characteristic (abbreviation, GMO) (166)
organismo modificado genéticamente un organismo que contiene material genético que ha sido alterado en forma artificial para producir una característica deseada (abreviatura: OMG)

genetic engineering (juh•NET•ik en•juh•NEER•ing)
a technology in which the genetic material of a living cell is modified (160)
ingeniería genética tecnología por la cual se modifica el material genético de las células vivas

© Houghton Mifflin Harcourt

mutation (myoo•TAY•shuhn)
a change in the nucleotide-base sequence of a gene or DNA molecule (84)
mutación un cambio en la secuencia de la base de nucleótidos de un gen o de una molécula de ADN

natural selection (NACH•uhr•uhl sih•LEK•shuhn)
the process by which individuals that are better adapted to their environment survive and reproduce more successfully than less well-adapted individuals do; a theory to explain the mechanism of evolution (99)
selección natural el proceso por medio del cual los individuos que están mejor adaptados a su ambiente sobreviven y se reproducen con más éxito que los individuos menos adaptados; una teoría que explica el mecanismo de la evolución

protein (PROH•teen)
a molecule that is made up of amino acids and that is needed to build and repair body structures and to regulate processes in the body (80)
proteína una molécula formada por aminoácidos que es necesaria para construir y reparar estructuras corporales y para regular procesos del cuerpo

radiometric dating (ray•dee•oh•MET•rik DAYT•ing)
a method of determining the absolute age of an object by comparing the relative percentages or ratio of a radioactive (parent) substance and the stable (daughter) substance found in the object (13)
datación radiométrica método para determinar la edad absoluta de un objeto al comparar los porcentajes relativos o la proporción de una sustancia radiactiva (sustancia madre) y la sustancia estable (sustancia hija) que se encuentra en el objeto

speciation (spee•shee•AY•shuhn)
the formation of new species as a result of evolution (116)
especiación la formación de especies nuevas como resultado de la evolución

species (SPEE•sheez)
a group of organisms that are closely related and can mate to produce fertile offspring (116)
especie un grupo de organismos que tienen un parentesco cercano y que pueden aparearse para producir descendencia fértil

variation (vair•ee•AY•shuhn)
the occurrence of hereditary or nonhereditary differences between different individuals of a population (96)
variabilidad la incidencia de diferencias hereditarias o no hereditarias entre distintos individuos de una población

© Houghton Mifflin Harcourt

Index

Note: Italic page numbers represent illustrative material, such as figures, tables, margin elements, photographs, and illustrations. Boldface page numbers represent page numbers for definitions.

© Houghton Mifflin Harcourt

C

D

© Houghton Mifflin Harcourt

© Houghton Mifflin Harcourt

© Houghton Mifflin Harcourt

© Houghton Mifflin Harcourt

K

knockout mice, 167, *167*
Knowlton, Nancy, 125–126, *125*
K-Pg extinction, *35, 36, 37, 37, 44*
Kutchicetus, 33, 50

L

Lagomorpha, *115*
land fossils, 10
Language SmArts, 14, 107
 Analyze Soapberry Bug Evolution, 120
 Compare Mechanisms of Change in Species, 149
 Defend a Claim with Evidence, 60
 Explain Inferences from Fossil Record Evidence, 40
 Identify a Potential Disease for Gene Therapy, 172
 Illustrate the Flow of Genetic Information, 83
 Predict Causes of Speciation, 120
law of faunal succession, 12
law of superposition, 11–12
lemur, 117, *117,* 129
Leptocoris, 120
Lesson Self-Check, 23–25, 43–45, 63–65, 91–93, 111–113, 127–129, 155–157, 175–177
life
 analyzing evidence of, 28–33
 analyzing patterns in the number of life forms over time, 34–40
 evidence of history of, 28–33
living organisms, 6, 10, 12, 17, 29, 48, 51, 58, *58,* 173, 178
Loxodonta, 59
lupine, 98, *98*

M

Machu Pichu, 66, *66*
mammals
 characteristics of, 49
 evolution of, 115, *115*
 speciation of, 127, *127*
mammoth, *58, 59*
manta ray, 94, *94*
marianna fruit bat, *122*
marine fossils, 10, *10,* 17
Marsupialia, *115*
mass extinction, 18, 34, *35, 36,* 45
mastadon, *58, 59*
Meganeura fossil, 40
Mendel, Gregor, 143
Metaspriggina genus, 31
meteorite, 37
mice, 167, *167,* 177
microfossil, 51
mineralized fossil, *8*
minimum viable population (MVP), 123
Miocene, *59*
models/modeling
 of analysis of fossil record, 38–39
 of *Dorodon atrox,* 5
 geologic columns, 12
 of microfossils, 51
 natural selection, 99
 using, 15
Moeritherium, 59
mold fossil, 6, *7*
monarch butterfly, *122*
Mongolian gerbil, 97, *97*
Monotremata, *115*
Morrison Formation, *8*
mosquito, 167, *167*
mosquito fossil, 4
Mount Burgess, Canada, 28
mountain goat, 88
mouse, 75, *75*
mouse embryo, 46
multicellular organisms, 31, *31*

M (continued)

museum exhibit designer, 61–62
mutagen, 84, 89
mutation, 73, 84–85, *84*
 adaptation and, 87–88
 phenotype and, 89–90
MVP (minimum viable population), 123

N

natural selection, 73, 75, 94–108, **99**, 143
 evolution and, 102–104
 modeling, 99-101
 populations change over time, 99–101, 112
 variation in populations, 96
natural system, 48
Neogene Period, *115, 121*
nine-banded armadillo, 96, *96*
nucleotides, 79, *79*
nucleus of cell, *78*

O

OCA2 gene, 160
ocelot, *88*
Oligocene, *59*
online activities, Explore ONLINE! 5, 23, 48, 99, 162
Opabinia, 30
Ordovician Period, *121*
Ordovician-Sulurian extinction, *35, 36, 44, 121*
Orthoceras, 35
overproduction, 102, 103
owl, *102*
ozone layer, 86, *86*

© Houghton Mifflin Harcourt

© Houghton Mifflin Harcourt

© Houghton Mifflin Harcourt